A Spiritual Theology of the Priesthood

A
SPIRITUAL THEOLOGY
OF
THE PRIESTHOOD

*The Mystery of Christ and
the Mission of the Priest*

Dermot Power

With a Foreword by
Robert Faricy SJ

T&T CLARK
EDINBURGH

T&T CLARK LTD
59 GEORGE STREET
EDINBURGH EH2 2LQ
SCOTLAND

First published 1998
Reprinted 1998

ISBN 0 567 08595 3

British Library Cataloguing-in-Publication Data
A catalogue record for this book is available from the British Library

Typeset by Rowland Phototypesetting Ltd, Bury St Edmunds, Suffolk
Printed and bound in Ireland by ColorBooks, Dublin

CONTENTS

FOREWORD

Here is a book about priesthood: a spirituality, a spiritual theology, of Christian priesthood. Father Dermot Power has created a spirituality of priesthood that synthesizes and builds on the theology of his mentor and friend Hans Urs von Balthasar, Pope John Paul II's favorite theologian and one regarded by many as the most important theologian of the twentieth century. In particular, Father Power shows us how priesthood is rooted in the mystery of Jesus Christ, in the mystery of his person, his life, his death and resurrection, and in the mystery of his presence with us.

This is a book to be read and pondered and prayed through by priests. And not only by priests. Every baptized Christian has a share in the priesthood of all Christians. And so every Christian can well profit from the spirituality found here.

Christian priesthood is a mystery. A threefold mystery: the priesthood of Jesus Christ, the priesthood of all Christians, and the ordained sacramental priesthood. While the spirituality brought forth in this book is principally that of the ordained priesthood, that same sacramental priesthood shares in a special way of course in the priesthood of Jesus Christ. And, naturally, it has a special relationship with the priesthood of all the faithful, while remaining distinct but certainly not separate from that broader and more extended priesthood.

All theology, and this includes spiritual theology, tries to bring to contemporary expression the word of God. This is a mysterious endeavor, because theology deals with the Christian mystery, and with its various parts or aspects, diverse Christian mysteries.

A mystery is a truth that we can never fully understand (because it participates in some way in the mystery of God himself), but that we can always understand more fully. We enter into a Christian mystery with our understanding, but we never finish. If I fully understand the mystery of Christian priesthood, then I must have missed something, I took a wrong turn somewhere, and what I understand is no longer Christian priesthood but something else.

Theology asks the question, 'What is priesthood?' Theology wants to describe the intelligibility of the concept 'priesthood.' What does 'priet' mean? What does 'priesthood' mean?

Spirituality goes further along that line of understanding; it asks not simply, 'What is a priest?' but beyond that, 'What does it mean to be a priest?' And, even further, 'How do I, how can I, live out my priesthood?'

Priesthood is not just something I do, but what I am. I not only do priesthood; I *am* a priest. Beyond my activity, priesthood belongs to my existence. Christian tradition expresses this by holding that priesthood is indelible. Like Melchisedek in the Old Testament, a Christian priest is a priest forever. Not just a profession, priesthood is a way of life, a life.

Dermot Power presents us here with a priestly spirituality for our times, a spirituality for every priest who belongs to a sacramental and hierarchical church. A spirituality, then, for every priest in union with the Roman Catholic Church as well as for priests in other Christian communions such as the Anglican Church, the Episcopalian Church, the Coptic Church, and all the orthodox churches.

Priestly spirituality is practical. This is its point: to help me to better live as a priest, to better live out my priesthood, today, in the world and in the times that I inhabit. Father Dermot gives us here just the book for that.

Robert Faricy SJ
Rome, Italy
November 23, 1997
Feast of Christ the King

PREFACE

The ministerial priesthood is in a very real sense living in an in-between time – it could be said that in recent decades it has moved from one extreme to another. On the one hand it was frozen into a mould that had to do with a rather rigid scholasticism where an underdeveloped ontology of priesthood failed to capture the imagination and where priestly character remained a rather arid and static notion, subsequently easily jettisoned to what became another extreme, that of mere function and a sociological principle of leadership in the community.

The frantic, well-intentioned and in some ways necessary embrace of developmental psychology and the behavioural sciences to meet the human and spiritual vacuum in priests' lives often had very little real baptism into the Christian mysteries of faith, hope and love which is a treasure that necessarily dwells in the earthenware jars of our institutional and personal fragilities.

This work inspired by the Christology of Hans Urs von Balthasar is intended to address the need of this transient moment and whilst not in any way searching to fill a vacuum, simply points in a direction that might begin to feed the spiritually hungry heart of the ministerial priest.

I would like to thank His Eminence Cardinal Basil Hume, Father Robert Faricy SJ, Father Herbert Alphonso SJ, the Reverend Dr Peter Burrows, Sister Alphonsus LSU and Stratford Caldecott for their support and encouragement over the years of writing and preparing this contribution to the spirituality of the ministerial priesthood.

While this office is definitely not the center, it must be rooted and maintained *in* the center, to become the criterion, the concrete point of reference for unity (and without it unity would fall apart), thus leading beyond itself to *the* center, Christ, and liberating people for Christian freedom. In this official role of the 'self-effacing', 'unworthy servant' who 'only does his duty' and expects no thanks for it (Lk 17:9–10), Peter becomes the prototype of all Christian living within the constellation of unity. This *renunciation* which lies at the heart of Catholic office is not primarily an ethical achievement but is intrinsic to its structure. The office-bearer is bound to exercise an office that is not his own; essentially he directs attention to someone else who 'leads him where he does not wish to go'; such an office can only be accepted with 'grief' (Jn 21:17) about one's unworthiness.

Hans Urs von Balthasar
The Office of Peter and The Structure of the Church
(San Francisco: Ignatius Press, 1986), p. 287

INTRODUCTION

It is the purpose of this study to explore the foundations of a spirituality of the ministerial priesthood in the light of the Christology of Hans Urs von Balthasar. At the outset it is worth noting that the whole of Balthasar's theological endeavour has to do with establishing the Christ-centre at the heart of all Christian reality and interpretation. In the context of a spiritual theology of priesthood, the Christology of Balthasar uncovers both the Christological depths of Christian priesthood and the power and richness of Catholic tradition that has constantly sought to interpret the priesthood in the light of the mystery of Christ.

The concern to affirm the Christ-centre at the heart of Christian reality was indeed a striking feature of Balthasar's own life and witness as a theologian and priest.[1] Hans Urs von Balthasar was born in Lucerne, Switzerland, in 1905, and died at his home in Basle in 1988. Educated both by Benedictines and Jesuits, Balthasar imbibed the traditions of Catholic thought and culture which, together with his encounters with Rudolph Allers, the disciple and critic of Freud; the great Protestant theologian Karl Barth; Erich Przywara; and the theologians of the 'Nouvelle Theologie', Henri de Lubac and Jean Daniélou, provided the theological awakenings and horizons which shaped and moulded his own search for a theological synthesis. Whilst Balthasar drew deeply from the Fathers of the Church, he also valued the theological sources he found in the world of art, literature and music. His whole theological witness was to the original unity and wholeness of all things in Christ. In particular he sought to highlight this truth for Christian spirituality.

It was my particular joy and privilege to have known Balthasar in the later years of his life; conversations with him and subsequent correspondence on the spirituality of ministerial priesthood enabled me to perceive clearly the need to connect priestly ministry directly and explicitly with the central mysteries of faith, and in particular the twin doctrines of the Incarnation and the Trinity. Balthasar's ecclesial method was concerned constantly to integrate the institutional dimensions of the Church's life with the depths of her essential mystery, as Christ's Body and Bride. This horizon for understanding priestly life

---

1 An exhaustive German bibliography under the title *Hans Urs von Balthasar: Bibliographie 1925–1990* is available from Johannes Verlag Einsiedeln.

and service became the stimulus for developing the major themes of this study.

The concern to develop a Christ-centred model of priestly spirituality is in no sense in opposition or indeed tension with the perception of ministerial priesthood as essentially a dimension of ecclesial reality. It is the clear teaching of Vatican II that the ministerial priesthood is a function within the Church, a service that exists primarily for the upbuilding of the community of faith, the People of God, the Church, the Body and Bride of Christ. At the same time this function is understood as moving along the lines of the fundamental ecclesial mystery which is the love of Christ for the Church, and not on any merely sociological or empirical interpretation of ministry as leadership or as functional role.

With Balthasar we have a theological method that conceives the whole enterprise of interpreting ecclesial reality as essentially tracing the contours of the Christ-Form, Trinity, Christology and Ecclesiology constituting an inseparable unity. Throughout this study we shall approach the place and meaning of the ordained minister within the Church through the prism of Balthasar's theological synthesis. We hope in so doing to provide a basis for a spirituality that holds together both the ecclesial and personal dimensions of priestly existence.

Just as Christology stands at the centre of Balthasar's Ecclesiology, it in turn has its own centre – the Cross. For Balthasar the event of the Cross discloses the extent to which God gives his Son out of love for the world, and the unconditionality with which the Son understands and accepts himself to be given.

And it is precisely this stance, taken by the Son towards the Father and for the Father's sake towards the world, that constitutes the Priesthood of Christ which in its twofold transcendence towards the Father and towards the world, continues in the Church. For Balthasar it is the obedient love of the Son towards the Father that is the mode of his priestly office, and it is only within the Form of this redemptive love that the continuation of the office of priesthood in the Church can be correctly perceived and understood.

This present work is an attempt to explore fundamental areas of priestly spirituality in the light of Balthasar's Christological method, which uncovers the Christological depths of the ministerial priesthood. Jesus is the prototype of Priesthood who has realised the full willingness to be given to the Father in the Holy Spirit; and at the same time this foundational act of Jesus' whole existence is the enabling ground and norm of every relationship in the Church. In the specific area of ministerial priesthood, Balthasar writes of priestly office as a transparency to the love of Christ for the Church. It has no other function than to represent this love of Christ. As Office, priesthood exists only to reflect and to serve this mystery. The event that grounds this fact cannot be interpreted in just any arbitrary sort of way; it has a distinctive form, the Form of the Self-giving of the Son in its Trinitarian depth. For Balthasar it is not possible for ministerial priesthood to develop its identity and mission from its own resources. It is only from these Christological depths that priesthood can find its full identity and meaning.

The interpenetration of the theory and praxis of priestly spirituality is reflected in the structure of this present work itself, which attempts to integrate the deepest Christological insight of Balthasar's theology with the challenges and needs of the presbyterate in this moment of its development and self-understanding.

Chapter I outlines briefly the Catholic consciousness of priesthood which is presupposed in this study, and is the *Sitz im Leben* of Balthasar's theology of priesthood. We then move on towards outlining the contours of a Christ-centred spirituality of ministerial priesthood, assessing its biblical foundations and reflecting on its consequences for contemporary priestly existence. Throughout this chapter we rely on Balthasar's theological method to uncover the Christological depths we are seeking to appropriate into the framework of a spiritual theology.

Chapter II takes up the identity of Christ as both Priest and Victim, examines Balthasar's treatment of this theme and explores more fully the complex Christological ideas that are intrinsic to the Christian image of priesthood and sacrifice, and that constitute the heart of Balthasar's own Christological endeavour. We shall pay special attention to the language of kenosis and expiation which are problematic for theology in general, and have been largely abandoned in contemporary theology of priesthood. We shall explore Balthasar's elucidation of the distinctive character of the sacrifice and Cross of Jesus, which for him can never be lost sight of in the authentic interpretation of Christian and ecclesial reality. The consequences of recovering this language for a spirituality of priesthood will be examined.

Chapter III will seek to show how, in Balthasar's Christology, the Cross as revelation of God's Trinitarian love is also the basis for an understanding of the mystery of the Church. Here Balthasar meditates upon the patristic idea of the nuptial consciousness of the Church, the Bride and Body of Christ, which for him is an image that illumines the place and meaning of the priestly office. Through this chapter we shall move through Balthasar's own unique ecclesial synthesis in which he interweaves what he calls the Christological constellation of Mary,

Peter and John with the continuing interpretation of ecclesial relation-ships. Here we find the meaning of the fragmented institutional office of priesthood in the light of the love of Christ crucified. It is an image of priesthood that mirrors its present experience of crisis while setting it within the context of the Paschal mystery. It is fundamentally an image of hope.

Chapter IV develops the idea of a Christological constellation by focusing on the Pauline paradigm of Office. Through the prism of Paul's ministry Balthasar perceives the key to integrating interiority and mission, identity and service which are at the heart of the contem-porary issues of priestly spirituality. Moving through to Paul's witness, we shall examine the need to recover a sense of identity with Christ in the praxis of priesthood and ask whether there is a place in contem-porary spirituality for a language of priestly character. Finally we shall reflect on the priesthood as a gift to the Church and situate the meaning of the Grace of Orders in the context of the mission of the Church.

In Chapter V we shall specify how, in Balthasar's vision, the spirit of the Evangelical Counsels sets the pastoral and spiritual life of the priest within the radicalism of the Gospel, and how this insight articu-lates all that *Pastores Dabo Vobis* presents to the presbyterate as its continuing ideal. In particular we shall explore the personal dimensions of holiness and consecration in the life of the ministerial priest as essentially a pastoral asceticism and how Balthasar comes to appreciate this medial position of the priesthood at the place where Church and world intersect as a place of kenosis, where the priest is configured to Christ the Good Shepherd who lays down his life. Balthasar, in his insistence that the priesthood is a state of life, believes that it is only in fully embracing the objectivity of his office that the priest can truly find and be most completely himself. How this ideal of spirituality is relevant to the lifestyle and ministry of priests will be assessed.

In Chapter VI we shall apply the principles of Balthasar's Christolog-ical and ecclesial synthesis to the specific area of the spirituality of the ministerial priesthood, in which priesthood comes to expression in its fully pastoral aspect. In Catholic life and tradition diocesan or secular priests are called to live out concretely and existentially the mystery of incarnate and redemptive love in the midst of the community of faith. The pattern of their lives is that of the Good Shepherd who lays down his life for his sheep. In the light of Balthasar's spiritual theology, the spiritual journey of the ministerial priest becomes the way of kenosis and of humble presence. The charism, then, of the pastoral priesthood is that the priest, through his presence with and to his people, mediates the redemptive mission of the Incarnate Son of God.

The purpose of this chapter is to take each of the classical functions of the ministerial priest and to view them in the light of Balthasar's creative insights. We shall look at the role of the priest as Shepherd, President, Teacher and Prophet, Reconciler and Mystic, and show in what sense these dimensions of his life and ministry are intimately linked to the mysteries of the Lord's own ministry and mission.

Chapter VII finally recapitulates the main features of a Christ-centred Spirituality of ministerial priesthood, but from within the context of the mystery of Divine Election and its apparent paradox of particularity where some are called for the sake of all. This is an entirely appropriate climax of the study in so far as it reflects the goal of all Balthasar's endeavours in his Christological enquiry, which is to plumb the depths of Jesus' identity and Trinitarian origin in its essential mystery of a love given for all, especially the lost and those forsaken by God. By delineating the lines of divine election from its origin in Israel to its outpouring as love for all, we shall try to situate the ministry of priestly service as love of Christ through the Church for the world. Drawn into the love of Christ by office and through discipleship, the priest is also part of the outreach of that love; keeping the twofold dimension alive is the purpose of a spiritual theology of priesthood for which the study of theology has attempted to lay some foundation. The purpose of this chapter is to engage with the whole question of the interpretation of the priesthood and indeed of the nature of the Church as such in the light of the subtle eclipse of sacred tradition in the contemporary search for a hermeneutic of Christian presence and ministry in the world. In retrieving the power and dynamic of sacred tradition for the interpretation of ecclesial reality Balthasar reaches into the heart of the crisis of priestly identity and illumines its depths and its darkness.

From this brief outline it is clear that it is not within the intention or scope of this study to enter directly into the vast area of controversy that surrounds the theology of priesthood at the present time. What is intended, however, is to provide a theological horizon to situate the question and issue of identity, lifestyle and future development that seem to characterise the present discussion within theology and spirituality of priesthood today. Nonetheless, we shall endeavour to address the facts of the issue implicitly and to enter into a respectful and critical dialogue along the way within a contemporary paradigm of priestly spirituality that perhaps may not reflect the specific presuppositions that underpin this study.

The title itself of this study indicates that what we are seeking to establish are the foundations of a spirituality of the ministerial priesthood. As such, the ministerial priesthood is exercised both by priests who belong to the local church or diocese and by priests who belong to religious orders or congregations. The focus in this study will be on the specific concerns of the diocesan priesthood, and more particularly as it exists in the part of the universal Church which is predominantly Western and urban, which is a factor that obviously nuances the life-style and the issues of the presbyterate serving in cities and in largely post-Christian societies.

The focus of this study reflects too a growing perception among commentators that the resolution to the present crisis facing the ministerial priesthood cannot remain solely at the level of spiritual or developmental issues, but must rediscover archetypes and original models of vocation and identity if the process of trial and dysfunction is to become a journey towards transformation and integrity.[2] This requires a theological method that can bear both the imaginative and spiritual weight of such an enterprise. It is in this area that Balthasar has a profound contribution to make. The present movement towards a new synthesis for the priesthood can be greatly enriched by the images of Balthasar's Christology, and particularly his theology of the Cross. These have provided not only mirror images for priests to find in their broken selves the icon of the crucified one, by whose wounds they can be healed, but also a language that can interpret the most painful, if not destructive, experiences of failure and futility as moments of disclosure of the God who in Balthasar's enlightening words, without leaving His own side, comes over to us in order to open up a way for us through the experiences of hopelessness and helplessness that would otherwise seem to lead only to abandonment, by God or of God.

Balthasar, too, offers a language that makes it possible for priests to come to love the Church and not merely to engage with ecclesial reality as an organisation or mere structure. Uncovering the Christolog-ical principles that lie at the heart of the pastoral and ecclesial ministry is ultimately not only then a matter of arriving at an authentic interpretation of priesthood, but is the basis of the healing of its wounds, the restoration of its identity and the inspiration for its praxis and mission.

Since his death in 1988, there has been an ever-growing critical appreciation of the achievement of Hans Urs von Balthasar in his theological and spiritual synthesis of the central mysteries of the Chris-tian faith. Underlying this analysis of his work has been the close

---

2 A good example of this recent trend in contemporary writing on the priesthood is the fascinating and challenging work by the American theologian and psychotherapist, William D. Perri. *A Radical Challenge for Priesthood Today* (Mystic, Conn.: Twenty-Third Publications, 1996).

attention given to the decisive and determining sources for the funda-mental shape of his own life and thought which in turn gave 'form' to his theological vision and insights. These sources range from his earliest academic interest in German idealism and apocalyptic through to his profound grasp of patristic theology, Christian spiritual tradition and the issue of what precisely Christian involvement and presence in the world entails. The encounters with other great theologians and Christian thinkers, including Erich Przywara, Karl Barth and Henri de Lubac have been well documented and examined. What most con-cerns the focus of this study, however, is the horizon that Balthasar's own life and experience as a priest and theologian gives to our under-standing of his theology and spirituality of the priesthood which, as we shall discover, reflects so much of what he actually lived himself.

Balthasar himself, at his first Mass, chose the words of the Eucharistic Consecration: *Benedixit, fregit, deditque* to symbolise his personal appro-priation of the meaning of priestly ministry. The narrative of his own priestly life and journey can certainly be read as an unfolding of this mystery. The breaking point of his own identity as a member of the Society of Jesus and the unexpected mission with the mystic Adrienne von Speyer led to his living on the margins of ecclesiastical life as a diocesan priest, but never in a parish; a theologian who never was to hold a chair of theology; a theological genius of the twentieth century in the Catholic tradition who was never invited to participate at the Second Vatican Council. The enigma, too, of a diocesan priest commit-ted wholly to the work of founding a community centred on the Beloved Disciple being led at the end of his days to the Petrine honour of the cardinalate, has been aptly described as a final fracture by Peter Henrici, SJ in his intimate account of Balthasar's life and mission.[3] These experiences are a thread of meaning that run through the whole of his life and experience and help situate what later would become the great themes of his theological reflection on the underlying sacri-ficial nature of the ministerial priesthood.

Like Bernanos' figure of the Curé in the *Diary of a Country Priest*, the priest in Balthasar's writing moves on the level of an empowerment that is at once both loving and hidden in its depth. These depths out of which the priest lives are mysterious, not easily probed by the tools of empiricism and not containable in simply sociological terms. In this we find the legacy of Adrienne and her insights into the unfolding of mystical experience in and through the concrete forms of all ecclesial

3 Cf. Peter Henrici, 'Hans Urs von Balthasar: A Sketch of His Life', *Communio*, XVI (1989), pp. 306–350.

life and service. Likewise, in Balthasar's wholehearted embrace of the Evangelical Counsels as the norm of the priestly state of life, we find the nuances of his own deep attachment to the religious life and to the spirit of the Society of Jesus which continued to sustain him for the whole of his life. The fact, too, that as a diocesan priest he lived within and for a community certainly colours his thinking about the priesthood and its place in the Church. These characteristics that are uniquely Balthasar's provide both gifts and limits to his work as a viable spiritual theology for the ministerial priesthood in this present moment of its development and self-understanding. It becomes one of our tasks, then, both to highlight the contribution that Balthasar has to make and to assess where his theological method perhaps fails in some ways to address the realities and challenges facing priestly identity and self-understanding.

This ambiguity emerges clearly in Balthasar's highly personal account of the theological mission he shared with Adrienne to recover the vitality and significance of the life of the Counsels for Christian discipleship and particularly the ministerial priesthood. This vision is outlined in *Unser Auftrag: Bericht und Entwurf*,[4] in which Balthasar assesses both his own and Adrienne's theological and spiritual insights into the nature and identity of the priesthood. Without doubt Balthasar believes that the development of the spirituality of the secular or diocesan priest, without explicit reference to the whole ambit of the life of the Counsels, most specifically obedience and poverty, is to be understood as a concession on behalf of the Church. He considers the rather notional assent to obedience in terms of a canonical relationship with the Bishop and the vague connection with poverty in the lifestyle of priests as an ambiguity that robs the pastoral vocation of the shepherd of its cutting edge.[5] Balthasar holds that precisely the exposure of the priest in his public and ministerial office, rather than diminishing the need for the radicalism of the Gospel, requires a very close identity with the life of the Counsels. Balthasar strongly refutes any suggestion that he is trying to turn diocesan priests into canonical religious[6] and rests his argument on the integration within tension that is an essential structure of the Mary-Peter-John relationship within the Church. Objective pastoral office needs constantly to connect with the realms of holiness and love in which its authority is rooted. For Balthasar the

4 Hans Urs von Balthasar, *Unser Auftrag: Bericht und Entwurf* (Einsiedeln: Johannes Verlag, 1984).
5 Ibid., p. 153.
6 Ibid., p. 113.

essential hermeneutic of priestly office is the question put to Peter, 'Do you love me, Peter? . . . Then feed my sheep.'[7]

While leaving the ministerial priesthood free from the limits and boundaries of subjectivity, Balthasar believes that this spirituality guarantees the boundlessness of pastoral love, which is the love of Christ for his Church and which constitutes the objectivity of office. What, however, cannot be given is the precise and pragmatic process by which the priest as person can come to appropriate the integration in tension of person and office that becomes the task of authentic priestly spirituality. Balthasar's estimation of his own thinking is that he provides a way of access into the depths of Christian and ecclesial experience, and it is a constructive one.

Another perception of priestly ministry might find in the intensity of Balthasar's conviction a weight of a tradition too heavy to bear and conclude that he is asking more of pastoral ministry than is essentially required. Ironically, Balthasar would probably accept this judgement and would argue that this is an appropriate place for priestly ministry to take its stand. It is essentially to do with the humiliation and risk of office, a function of which is to serve as a foil for the greater paradox of grace which chooses and shines through what is humanly weak.

The question needs to be addressed as to whether Balthasar offers merely an idealised and romantic account of the ministerial priesthood that evades the urgency of new and pragmatic approaches to contemporary issues surrounding ministry or does he in fact provide a breakthrough in vision and in insight into a level of interpretation and transformation for priestly ministry that more pragmatic models of spirituality fail to reach. This question permeates and underlies the critical stance that this study seeks to bring both to uncovering the presuppositions of Balthasar's own nuanced position in regard to the priesthood and to the corresponding presuppositions of those who seek an equation for the shape and direction of the priesthood that does not give such weight as Balthasar does to the dynamic and claims of tradition.

A critical assessment of these theological styles and positions which tend to set Balthasar apart from other contemporary Catholic theologians might, in fact, reveal an openness and vulnerability in his theological method to the more radical features of Christian revelation, in particular the Trinitarian drama of God's loving involvement with the world which can never leave the question of Christian presence and ministry at the level of the merely functional. In fact, it could be

---

7 Ibid., p. 155.

argued that Balthasar's hesitation or indeed inability to address explicitly the more concrete, socio-historical issues surrounding the shape of ministry in the contemporary world has sharpened his articulation of the abiding and normative content of the mysteries of faith. Even if this detachment is seen and judged to be an inherent weakness in his method, his apparent neglect of the concrete need not eclipse his theological achievement in refusing to move away from the centre, the Christ-centre, which at all times permeates and directs his theological enquiry and elucidation. We shall attempt, then, to present the coherency and consistency of Balthasar's theology of the priesthood in such a way as to distil from his magisterial synthesis those insights which provide the necessary link between the mysteries of faith and personal and ministerial experience that the Church believes constitutes her priesthood, its meaning and its mission.

I

THE MINISTERIAL PRIESTHOOD IN THE LIGHT OF THE MYSTERY OF CHRIST

INTRODUCTION

This chapter explores the foundations of a spirituality of the ministerial priesthood in the light of the mystery of Christ, with a special reliance on the theological methodology of Balthasar, whose constant concern is to uncover the depths of the whole of Christian and ecclesial reality. This concern is currently at the heart of the debate within the Church on the meaning and place of the ministerial priesthood. It is certainly at the centre of the theological underpinning of *Pastores Dabo Vobis*, in which the Holy Father recovers the Christological principle which has from the very beginning directed Catholic tradition in its understanding of the priesthood. This Christological principle, however, can never be treated in isolation from an understanding of the community of faith which is endowed with a variety of gifts of the Spirit which include other forms of ministry. An authentic theology of the priesthood can only be developed within a total ecclesiology which embraces both the Christological and the pneumatological, the ontological and the functional, a task which challenges our use of the language of priesthood to correspond and not to distort the essential paradigms of both the ecclesial and the Gospel tradition from which Catholic consciousness understands itself dynamically to unfold. The pluralism of post-Conciliar theology, especially in relation to the ordained ministry, needs to be held in focus as we explore Balthasar's own theological agenda, which does not always identify explicitly with ongoing reflection on priesthood that may contrast with his own. This tendency to operate outside of an engagement with other contemporary strands of theological thinking is a characteristic of Balthasar's overall theological approach which can at times rob his insights of a critical cutting edge that might have come from a more dynamic dialogue within his methodology. The epistemological significance of this missing dimension cannot, however, eclipse Balthasar's commitment to uncovering the full extent of the divine involvement with the world as the horizon for the Church's own presence and ministry in the world. In particular, Balthasar allows for the continuing question to be asked as to how Christ's priestly activity on behalf of the Father's love for the world can be related to the concrete mission of the ordained ministry. To ask this question of the ordained priesthood opens up for ministerial understanding a significance for its place, not only for the Church, but for the salvation of the world that theologies which cannot sustain such a question fail to hold out.

It is appropriate that at the beginning of this work we should engage with the language and images of priesthood in the light of wider questions, not only to do with ecclesial structure, but of the Kingdom and of the world. This again is one of the strengths of Balthasar's relentless theological endeavours which was always to uncover the Trinitarian and Christological depths of Christian life and ministry and to see here the roots, the framework and the guiding principle of its boundless, liberating and wholly concrete engagement with the world. While these Trinitarian and Christological starting points might hinder Balthasar's full embrace of the starting points of pastoral and social concerns which have become urgent questions for the structure and scope of priestly ministry in today's Church and world, this hesitancy can be understood more in terms of personal sensibilities to do with the background and lifesetting of Balthasar's formation and role as a theologian than with any intrinsic failure *per se* of his theological method to engage with the concrete realities that pastoral ministry inevitably entails.

Rather, the Christological themes and scope of Balthasar's reflection may be seen to be taking seriously the realities of our broken world and that in uncovering these profound Christological principles and showing them to be at the very heart of Christian ministry, Balthasar forges new and radically original categories for interpreting the priesthood in the light of the mystery of Christ.

We begin by outlining the main presuppositions of our enquiry, and in particular, the Catholic consciousness of priestly ministry and identity, its roots in tradition and its present stage of development within the self-understanding of the Church. We then attempt to place the Christological methodology of Balthasar within the various contexts and debates of contemporary theology of priesthood that are both firmly rooted in the biblical witness and able still to sustain an authentic vision and praxis for priesthood in our own time.[1]

1 For a comprehensive survey of these contemporary debates, cf. Patrick J. Dunn, *Priesthood; A Re-examination of the Roman Catholic Theology of the Presbyterate* (New York: Alba House, 1990).

AN ENDURING STRUCTURE

We begin by establishing the precise *Sitz im Leben* of our inquiry, which might best be described as a vision of ministerial priesthood within the boundaries of an ecclesial consciousness that has its roots in Catholic tradition and which rests upon the twin axioms of that tradition – that when we speak of Christian priesthood, we are thinking of the unique and definitive Priesthood of our Lord Jesus Christ and its continuation in the priesthood of All the Faithful who together participate in his holiness and redemptive love, through the office and service of ministerial priesthood.

The richness of this interdependence as understood in Catholic tradition is expressed very clearly in a classical presentation by Père Joseph Lecuyer in *Le Sacerdoce dans Le Mystère du Christ*, where he writes:

One will remember that the hierarchical priesthood which represents the priesthood of the Head of the Mystical Body and its sacrament in the sense we have just explained, so far from excluding the priesthood of all the members of the Mystical Body, constantly presupposes that priesthood. The hierarchical priesthood is established for the functioning of the whole body which is the Church, and for the good of that body, so that all its members may actualise the spiritual sacrifice which gives them access, with Jesus, to the true sanctuary. It is, then, in union with all the baptised that the hierarchical priesthood offers the sacrifice of the Paschal Mystery, and with the collaboration of all the confirmed that is the New Covenant, it realises the apostolic mission of the new People of God.[2]

This theme is developed also by Louis Bouyer:

When we see the priest in the midst of his brothers in Christ celebrating the Eucharist with men, it should be manifest that this ministerial priesthood, the sacramental sign in our midst of the one priesthood of Christ, far from making useless or void the royal priesthood of all believers, has no other meaning or object but to make it fully actualized.[3]

---

2 Joseph Lecuyer, *Le Sacerdoce dans le Mystère du Christ* (Paris: 1957), quoted in author's translation in Aidan Nichols, OP, *Holy Order* (Dublin: Veritas, 1990), p. 131.
3 Louis Bouyer, 'The Priest and the Eucharist' in Robert E. Terwilliger and Urban T. Holmes III (ed.), *To Be A Priest* (New York: Seabury Press, 1975), p. 109.

In the Catholic tradition the distinction between the priesthood of All the Faithful and the ordained ministry is conceived as one that bestows unity and exists only for the sake of the holiness of all. In both its Christological and ecclesial foundation, the theology of the Second Vatican Council develops this twin axiom of Catholic tradition and especially in the documents *Lumen Gentium* and *Presbyterorum Ordinis*[4] which explore the intrinsic unity and correspondence between the two aspects of Christian priesthood.

Although other scholars have pointed to areas of theological inconsistency in the Council's treatment and assessment of the precise relationship between the ordained ministry and the priesthood of All the Faithful,[5] it is nevertheless clear that the intention of the Council was towards establishing the interconnection and dependence between the two. The function of the ministerial priesthood is understood in terms of service to the whole Church; building up the community in faith and love; a dynamic within the Church that is not a status but a responsibility; and a gift to the whole Church, continuing the ministry of Christ himself who loved the Church and gave himself up for her.[6]

This identification of the office of ministerial priesthood with the continuation of Christ's presence in the Church, as a distinctive participation in his redemptive mission, different in kind but not in degree, has long been the subject of theological debate.

While it may be true to suggest, as many theologians have, that the way in which the Church has come to express this identification requires constant development and refinement,[7] it remains valid to hold as normative for the spirituality of priesthood the foundational theological insight of this close identification which the Council has fundamentally reaffirmed.

A thorough examination of the history of the development of priesthood in Catholic tradition reveals a constant searching to find an appropriate language to express this sense of identification with the ministry of Jesus himself.[8] Vatican II reaffirms the Christological foundations for ministry, declaring that Jesus himself is the basis of

4 *Lumen Gentium* and *Presbyterorum Ordinis: Vatican Council II*, A. Flannery, OP (ed.), (Collegeville: Liturgical Press, 1975).
5 A most thorough assessment of the Council's development of the theology and spirituality of ministerial priesthood is, Kenan B. Osborne, OFM, *Priesthood; A History of the Ordained Ministry in the Roman Catholic Church* (New York: Paulist Press, 1988).
6 Ibid., pp. 3–29.
7 Ibid., p. 315.
8 Ibid., p. 315.

ministry, and that to comprehend the meaning of all Christian ministry one must begin with the ministry of Jesus.[9]

According to *Presbyterorum Ordinis*, Jesus himself becomes the focus of the spirituality of priesthood; priests are configured to Christ the Priest. Although this is fully in keeping with the Conciliar teaching that all are called to holiness in Christ and that there is no particular holiness for the ordained minister which the unordained does not share in, the priest in his service to the Church has a configuration with Christ in his mission and ministry which obviously nuances his identity and spiritual life.[10]

Thus, while models of priestly existence were never 'frozen' into one particular mould in Catholic tradition, the common denominator in all its diversity was the Christological factor of identity with Christ, a closeness to Jesus Christ which provides the thread of spiritual identity that runs through the whole complex development of priesthood in Christian tradition.[11]

This thread of spiritual identity with Christ is what Jean Galot refers to as an 'enduring structure', which continues to mould and direct the self-understanding of Catholic priesthood, in providing it with its ultimate configuration and identity in Christ.[12]

There is a tendency in contemporary investigations into the foundations of priesthood in the New Testament, to question the possibility of any structural foundation to what later emerges as priesthood in the earliest community of faith. This is certainly the thesis of Edward Schillebeeckx, who separates the proclamation of the Gospel from the foundation of any seminal structure endowed with apostolic authority from the very beginning.[13] His case rests on a perception of the evidence that would suggest a process of choosing

9 Osborne observes that in the great Scholastic writers – Thomas, Bonaventure, Albert, Scotus – the actual ministry of Jesus played no role at all in their theology of priesthood. Vatican II, however, instructs us to see in the very mission and ministry of Jesus the foundation for all definition, description and spirituality of Church ministry. Ibid., p. 317.

10 Ibid., p. 334.

11 For a clear presentation of this Catholic theology of Order, cf. A. Vanhoye, 'Sacerdoce commun et sacerdoce ministériel: distinctions et rapports', *Nouvelle Revue Théologique*, 107: (1975), pp. 193–207.

12 Jean Galot, *Theology of the Priesthood*, ET (San Francisco: Ignatius Press, 1984), p. 86. Galot throughout this detailed study emphasises that it is in Christ himself that the priesthood of the New Covenant discerns its truth and possibilities. Consecration, service, shepherding and mission all have their foundation in the Eternal Priesthood of Christ himself.

13 E. Schillebeeckx, *Ministry: A Case for Change* (London: SCM Press, 1981); and 'The Christian Community and Its Office-holders', *Concilium*, 133 (1980), pp. 95–133.

leaders in the community by spontaneous acclaim without reference to the apostles who simply accepted them as a *fait accompli*. The implicit theological presupposition is that the ordained ministry was brought into being as something necessary for Church order but which did not relate to or inherit the apostolic ministry itself.

Judicious assessments of Schillebeeckx's interpretation of the origins of ministry[14] have raised certain questions about his selective use of Scripture and tradition in supporting the hypothesis that the development of the ordained ministry is more to be understood in accordance with the sociological principles of group formation and leadership than as a sacramentally and apostolically rooted continuation of the presence and power of the ministry of Jesus himself. The principle of Catholic tradition which Schillebeeckx and others forego in order to maintain this position grounds the ordained ministry in the very origins of Christianity and understands that in the apostles the Lord left to his community a ministry for the purpose of sanctifying, teaching and governing the Church, and that this apostolic ministry was not merely an organisational convenience, but a legitimate development of Christ's own ministry, a continuing gift to the Church.

Whereas the precise stages of this process of transmission and development cannot now be traced, it is possible to understand the growth of ministry of priesthood as already emerging in the New Testament within the dynamic of traditions whereby the seeds of the present consciousness of Holy Orders can be found in the soil of the New Testament from which the Christian priesthood has grown. The process whereby some features of Catholic faith, ethics and worship are regarded as legitimate outgrowths from New Testament origins may be described as an hermeneutic of recognition in which we who share the developed consciousness of the later Church, come to the evidence of the early Church.[15]

There seems to be an emergent polarisation between those who hold that Jesus himself instituted a structure/ministry to sustain the Church in its life and mission and those who perceive ministry to be the way in which the Church moved itself towards organising its own structure and ministry, in its freedom as a Spirit-filled and directed community of faith.[16]

14 Cf. Albert Vanhoye, 'Le ministère dans l'Église: Les données du nouveau testament', *Nouvelle Revue Théologique*, 104 (1982), p. 720; and Patrick J. Dunn, *Priesthood*, 'Chapter IV: The Writings of Edward Schillebeeckx', pp. 31–44.
15 For an elucidation of this place of the hermeneutic of recognition in Christian tradition, cf. Aidan Nichols, OP, *Holy Order*.
16 For an example of such polarisation, cf. Edmund Hill, OP, *Ministry and Authority in the Church* (London: Chapman, 1988).

In the light of the evidence of New Testament tradition and the whole development of hermeneutics and biblical theology, these options require a context that is perhaps more faithful to the original data of the New Testament witness itself. The continuing hermeneutic of recognition which is at the heart of the principles of Catholic tradition refers to that historical pattern of relationship, intimacy and mission which characterised Jesus' formation of the Twelve and became the pattern of association and the normative structure of meaning for subsequent interpretation of ministry and vision in his name. This perception of the 'dynamic' of tradition [17] moves away from any 'static' understanding of a Christ-centred theology of priestly ministry with an hermeneutic that is both founded in the tradition and open to the future.

Here we face the question of the very nature of all Christian existence, whether the life and ministry of Jesus is simply an example or whether it is in some sense to be understood as derivative of Christ's experience.[18] In the context of ministerial priesthood, a paradigm of priesthood that holds Christ simply as exemplar cannot engage with the question of how we are to relate the continuing presence and power of the Incarnate Lord to the Church's ministry to the world. If Christian theology cannot directly relate the institutional ecclesial ministry with the continuing presence and ministry of Jesus in the Church, then it is robbed of a dynamism that was certainly present in the New Testament which perceives the mission of, first the Twelve, and then later of Paul, as the prolongation of the primordial mission which the Son has received from the Father.

It is in relating the institutional and fragmented priesthood as a dimension and function of ecclesial life to the centre of faith, to the Christ-centre, that the Christological methodology of Balthasar has a contribution to make that is both enriching for priestly self-

---

17 Cf. Hans Urs von Balthasar, *Klarstellungen: zur Prufung der Geister* (Freiburg-im-Breisgau: Verlag Herder KG, 1971), English translation (abbreviated ET throughout footnotes) John Riches, *Elucidations* (London: SPCK, 1975), in which Balthasar explores the dynamic of tradition as an inexhaustible source of life and freedom for the Church. For Balthasar, it is precisely the pattern of relationship between Jesus and his Apostles that continues to provide the basis for the essential structure of Orders. Form and love, institution and spirit, structure and relationship are held in creative interplay through the dynamic of tradition.

18 Part of a larger Christological question which many authors today hold to be at the heart of the question of Christian credibility in the secular world. Cf. Hans Urs von Balthasar, *Wer ist ein Christ* (Einsiedeln: Johannes Verlag, 1965), ET *Who Is a Christian* (London, 1968); and Eric Mascall, *Theology and the Gospel of Christ* (London: SPCK, 1977); and Walter Kasper, *Theology and Church* (London: SCM Press, 1989); and John Macquarrie, *Jesus Christ in Modern Thought* (London: SCM Press, 1990).

understanding and relevant to contemporary theological debate. It also allows for a continual interpretation of the ministerial priesthood in the world which a model of priesthood that begins simply with an empirical, sociological interpretation of its meaning cannot sustain.

PRIESTHOOD – UNFOLDING FROM THE CHRIST-CENTRE

Balthasar's perception of Christian truth is that it is both 'symphonic' and 'catholic' in its wholeness: its worship, liturgy, ethics and pastoral dimensions unfold from the Christ-centre where all the leitmotifs of Christian living are re-orchestrated in an harmonious unity.[19]

Balthasar is always concerned, before and in all particular theological questions, to get a view of the 'whole' in Christian faith as such.[20] The one fundamental Christian mystery, i.e. God's love for the world in the gift of His Son and the sacrament of His Church, should be recognised in its original 'infold', so that it can also be continually recognised in its detailed unfolding, i.e. in the most varied expression of faith, sacramental, liturgical forms and structures of the community of faith.[21]

For Balthasar, then, the Church event stands in closest correlation with the Christ event,[22] and in this resides the context for understanding ministerial priesthood and its identity. By placing the institutional and ecclesial dimension of priesthood within the unfolding of the 'Christ-Form',[23] Balthasar opens up for the spirituality of ministerial priesthood, a theology of identity with Christ that might remain problematic for

---

19 Cf. Hans Urs von Balthasar, *Die Warheit ist Symphonisch* (Eisiedeln: Johannes Verlag, 1972).

20 In his introduction to Balthasar's theology, Medard Kehl provides us with a clear and comprehensive account of Balthasar's Christo-centric Ecclesiology. He describes several features of Balthasar's fundamental methodology which allows for each separate dimension of ecclesial life to be connected back to the centre of faith: the Christ-centre; cf. Medard Kehl and Werner Loeser (ed.), *The Von Balthasar Reader* (Edinburgh: T. and T. Clark, 1982), pp. 3–51.

21 Ibid., pp. 34–35, where Kehl describes the concern of Balthasar always to perceive the 'whole' before its parts, and to affirm the primordial unity which precedes every critical analysis or listing of the varied elements of faith.

22 Ibid., p. 37.

23 'Form' or 'Christ-Form' is used by Balthasar in the sense of the German *gestalt*, but with the added dimension of an almost 'archetypal' structure of things. It is the universally intended modelling of the human person after Christ which takes place initially in the Church. For a clear and precise treatment of this and other seminal ideas of Balthasar, see E. Oakes, *Pattern of Redemption* (New York: Continuum, 1991).

other theological models that have a starting-point other than his own, which is to emphasise the primacy of the 'Christ-Form' in all things.

This process is a matter of allowing the ecclesial dimension always to be turned back to its Christological origin and depths. When this takes place in the context of priesthood, we come to see it as a reality that ultimately unfolds from the 'Form' of Christ and his redemptive love for the Church. Since the 'Form' of Christ gives shape to all dimensions of Christian existence, it is not something unique to priesthood, but what it does is to distil what in Christian priesthood gives it its unique configuration to the person of Christ. For Balthasar, the priesthood exists only to make transparent the 'Form' of Christ's love for the Church, his Body and Bride, as a crystallisation of that love. It has no other function than to make that love transparent.

Furthermore, according to Balthasar, the historically conditioned and fragmented ministry of the Church cannot be open to mere empirical investigation, measured in terms of its apparent sociological function as leadership. There is a theological truth at stake here that somehow must be allowed to emerge at every point of interpretation. This truth has to do with the hidden 'Form' of the love of Christ for his Church, a nuptial consciousness that is at the deepest level of ecclesial life.

Throughout his ecclesiology, Balthasar focuses the Church's life in the presence of this nuptial consciousness of reciprocal love.[24] The Church, he says, shares in the twofold transcendence of Christ, towards the Father and towards the world, and is the locus of both disclosure and encounter with this transcendent love. In Balthasar's view, the Church cannot seek an autonomous form over against its Lord and his *gestaltung sufart* or 'Form'-giving Power.

This shaping power of love towards the Father and the world shapes the Church's presence in the world and grounds and motivates her involvement with society in the depths of the 'divine involvement'.[25]

24 For a detailed and explicit treatment of these themes of Ecclesiology, cf. Hans Urs von Balthasar, *Sponsa Verbi (=Skizzen zum Theologie II)* (Einsiedeln: Johannes Verlag, 1960), ET *Church and World*, trans. A. V. Littledale with A. Dru (New York: Herder and Herder, 1967); and *Herrlichkeit: Eine Theologische Aesthetik, Vol. I: Schau der Gestalt*; 2nd ed. (Einsiedeln: Johannes Verlag, 1967), ET *The Glory of the Lord, Vol. I: Seeing the Form* (Edinburgh: T. and T. Clark, 1982).
25 A Trinitarian vision of ecclesial involvement shared by many other theologians, and in particular, Jürgen Moltmann, *The Trinity and the Kingdom of God* (London: SCM Press, 1981); and *History and the Triune God* (London: SCM Press, 1991). Whilst Moltmann's emphasis is more 'political' and guided towards praxis, he shares common ground with Balthasar in his concern to recover the doctrine of the Trinity as the primal hermeneutic of Christian interpretation. Like Balthasar, Moltmann places the event of the Cross at the centre of Trinitarian theology.

The twofold transcendence of that divine involvement overcomes any polarisation between Church and world, revealing the boundlessness of Trinitarian love for the world which is at the heart of the 'Christ-Form' and its unfolding in ecclesial existence. Drawn into the orbit of Trinitarian love and its transcendence, Christian involvement becomes also part of the outreach of that love. In this most radical grasp of the profound depth of ecclesial consciousness, Balthasar uncovers for the priesthood of the Church contours that correspond with the original structure of Christian experience: The twofold transcendence between the Father and the world which is the Form of the Son's love and mission. The New Testament itself is 'controlled' by the hermeneutic of this twofold transcendence that characterises first Jesus' own self-understanding and self-interpretation and then subsequent interpretation of him.[26]

In terms of Catholic consciousness of ministerial priesthood, Balthasar's methodology allows for this Christological hermeneutic to have its full and normative 'control' on what we perceive priesthood to be in terms of both theory and praxis.

Uncovering this Christological depth of Christian priesthood brings to the fore a dynamic of priesthood that engages both with the interiority of spiritual identity in Christ and with a total involvement in the reality of the world. This twin solidarity with God and with the world, which dominates the whole of Balthasar's theological method, represents for him the very foundation of Christian reality.

How this hermeneutic unfolds in the ecclesial milieu of ordained ministry involves us in the whole area of the language and image of priesthood which has become an issue in contemporary theology. On the one hand, some exegetes point to the presence of priestly language in the New Testament witness as one of twin solidarity between God and ourselves, and in this understanding of the evidence there is a close correspondence between Balthasar's hermeneutic and the original New Testament data itself.[27] On the other hand, other theologians find problematic the apparent absence of any 'priestly' language in the Gospel tradition and question therefore the whole use of priestly

---

26 A view of New Testament hermeneutics proposed by the English theologian Robert Butterworth, SJ, in 'The Doctrine of the Trinity,' *The Way*, 24 (1984), where he explores the essential Christological structures of Christian reality.

27 An examination of this issue, taking to task the Catholic insistence on a priestly language for its office-holders, is J. D. G. Dunn, *The Parting of the Ways* (London: SCM Press, 1991), pp. 96ff. In his detailed examination of the New Testament data, Dunn perceives a radical parting with Old Testament ideas of cultic persons and sacred space which he believes has been downplayed in Catholic tradition.

language in relation to the ministry of Jesus and its continuation in the community of faith.[28]

How we resolve this issue which has been described as a 'thorny question' for Christian interpretation is pivotal for the validity of a spirituality of Christian ministry that finds its identity in the Priesthood of Christ.

THE LANGUAGE OF PRIESTHOOD – A THORNY QUESTION

In facing the 'thorny question' of the language of priesthood and its use in Christian theology, we have heard the view held by many theologians that it is impossible to trace 'priestly' contours from the Gospel witness to Jesus and that any subsequent investigation of priesthood in relation to ministry in his name has no valid biblical foundation. While these scholars accept the witness of the Epistle to the Hebrews to Christ's heavenly 'high priestly' role, any attempt to relate this role to continuing Christian ministry is thought by these scholars to be asking too much of the evidence.

That Balthasar is able to sustain a monumental Christology and Ecclesiology that presupposes a 'priestly' dimension to Jesus' life and mission, is an issue we must at least address, in so far as the issue underpins the whole argument and context of our study. Furthermore, since the whole onus of Catholic tradition is rooted in a consciousness of priesthood that is Christ-centred, the resolution of this question is not merely speculative, but essential for a living and authentic spirituality.

The resolution may lie in the specific line of enquiry that Balthasar, among others, believes to correspond more accurately to the data and original structure of the New Testament witness. It is best described as an indirect or implicit Christology, in which the post-Easter Christological titles and confessional testimonies about Jesus are understood to be an unforced development and explicit expression of an implicit experience and reality that have their origins in Jesus himself.[29]

The subsequent Christology of the New Testament is therefore conceived to be the translation and interpretation of what is already

---

28 Cf. Albert Vanhoye, SJ in *Old Testament Priests and the New Priest* (Petersham, Massachusetts: St Bede's Publications, 1986), pp. 39–59.

29 For a detailed exploration of indirect or implicit Christology, cf. Walter Kasper, *The God of Jesus Christ* (London: SCM Press, 1983), pp. 168ff.

present in Jesus' own experience, i.e. his obedience and self-surrender as Son; and that what Jesus lived out ontically before Easter is interpreted ontologically after Easter.[30]

Furthermore, an implicit Christology centres on certain features and fundamental structures of the New Testament which provide access to those original experiences of Jesus which led him to be described and understood in no less terms than those that relate to both God and man. The distinguished Anglican theologian and exegete C.D.F. Moule observes that this development of Christological language and title is not a matter simply of pious imaginations embroidering and enlarging the Person of Christ, but rather a consistent difficulty of how to reach any insight that would approach a description that was not pitifully inadequate.[31] Successive attempts at word painting did not evolve away from the original. They are all only inadequate representations of the original and unique figure that has been here from the beginning.

The development of Christology in the New Testament is thus to be understood as a sharpening and refinement of language to do justice to an original definitive experience of Jesus which remains normative for subsequent interpretation of him and the impact he made.[32]

Furthermore, the distinctiveness of Christian faith and revelation led from the very beginning to a judicious use of language, and especially of already existing religious categories. More often than not, the early Christians refrained from contemporary and functional language to do with divine realities in order to safeguard and promote what was radical and new to Christian reality and religious experience.[33]

In the specific area of the language and image of priesthood and its place in the New Testament, the exegete Albert Vanhoye has provided a most exact and comprehensive elucidation of the development of priestly language in biblical tradition.[34] He distinguishes between two interrelated layers of New Testament traditions. The first is the presence of a dimension of Jesus' original experience and ministry which in the process of reflection led to a second layer of a new and radical application of the religious category of priesthood which communicates the profound significance for continuing Christian interpretation of the original and derivative experience of Jesus himself. The absence of a

30 Ibid., pp. 173ff.
31 C.D.F. Moule, *The Origin of Christology* (Cambridge: University Press, 1977).
32 Cf. J.D.G. Dunn, *Jesus and the Spirit: A Study of the Religious and Charismatic Experience of Jesus and the First Christians as Reflected in the New Testament* (London: SCM Press, 1975); and *Christology in the Making* (London: SCM Press, 1980).
33 Cf. J. D. G. Dunn, *The Parting of the Ways*, pp. 75–95.
34 Albert Vanhoye, *Old Testament Priests and the New Priest*.

priestly language in the earlier tradition, and more specifically in the Gospel tradition, does not of necessity imply the absence of a priestly dimension in Jesus' life: What later led to a freedom and instinct in Christian consciousness to describe Jesus in priestly terms was a dimension which we shall see was always implicitly present in the life and attitude of Jesus himself.[35]

Some biblical scholars suggest that Jesus was not a Levite and did not belong to the priestly cult in Israel. His Priesthood, say these scholars, while realising the deepest longing of Israel's faith and cult, transcends its boundaries and limits in his twin solidarity between God and man that constitutes his humanity. The apparent absence of a cultic-priesthood language in the earliest tradition is accounted for by the concern to establish the definitive and radical revelation of God in Jesus and the ideal revelation of God that was made possible through him.[36]

This new and ideal access to God becomes the main *leitmotif* of the Epistle to the Hebrews, and Vanhoye, in his exegesis of its text[37] outlines the main features of the theology of the Priesthood of Christ that Hebrews formulates, not only in response to exigencies of the time and situation of a Church in obvious trial and crisis, but also as a stylised account and interpretation of the human experience of the historical Jesus that constitutes his eternal and eschatological office as High Priest.

Vanhoye shows how Hebrews recasts the Synoptic traditions about Jesus' inner life of prayer and surrender, his filial identity and its realisation in the crucible of suffering.[38]

Vanhoye, on the evidence and witness of Hebrews, delineates the distinctive lines of this new and radical priesthood, which has to do with the 'liturgy' of the human heart of Jesus, his real and concrete self-giving love to God and to others which takes on the mode of sacrifice.

Instead of a ritual ceremony, performed with the blood of an animal, there was involved a terribly real event of human history in which Jesus engages his whole person on the path of his obedience to God

---

35 Ibid., pp. 280ff.
36 Ibid., pp. 47–52.
37 Ibid., pp. 65–87.
38 Ibid., pp. 112ff. This view of the reliance of Hebrews on the Synoptic traditions of Jesus' filial identity and vulnerable humanity is shared by David Stanley, who attempts to demonstrate how clearly reliant Hebrews is on the tradition of the trial of Jesus and on the Synoptic Gethsemane narratives; cf. David Stanley, *Jesus in Gethsemane* (New York: Paulist Press, 1982).

and his self-offering to his brothers. In such a 'sacrifice', it was not an animal victim that had been initially sacrificed, but it was man himself, who in Jesus had been transformed in two ways at once: He had been raised to a new relationship with God in glory, and at the same time, he had acquired a new capacity for communion with other men. In this way the new covenant had been fulfilled.

Vanhoye highlights as the primary trait of the Priesthood of Christ in Hebrews precisely the twofold transcendence that Balthasar perceives to be at the heart of the whole New Testament Christology. At the same time he points to the emphasis on the dimension of compassion and the humility of Christ as an outstanding characteristic of the radical newness of New Testament priesthood.[39]

The basis for this new priesthood in the Synoptic tradition is in the attitude of Jesus towards the Father's will and his sense of solidarity with us. To the very end, Jesus carried out the will of his Father and manifested the boundless limits of his solidarity with us. Such was the attitude of Jesus that nothing was able to make him compromise either his union with the Father, or his bonds with us. In him these mutualities strengthen each other.[40]

Thus the later development of the language of priesthood can be understood to be in response to the most profound experiences and dimension of Jesus' life and ministry, experiences which ultimately led to the breakdown of familiar religious categories to do justice to the mysteries of divine involvement that characterise Christian faith. Christian reflection came to be involved in a process of recasting the most treasured images of Israelite faith, which came in time to include the image of priesthood.

Rather than being an image that is 'extrinsic' to authentic Christology and one that can in a contemporary word-picture of Christian reality be dispensed with, the language and images of priesthood capture something of the original vulnerability and existential self-giving of the historical Jesus, that from the origin of Christian reflection fulfilled the function of keeping that original mission alive at the heart of Christian worship and praxis.

By perceiving the title of 'priest' to be a later description of the vocation of Jesus, intelligible, however, in the setting of his own life and ministry, we are firmly rooted in a Christological line of enquiry

39 On the humility of Christ, cf. Hans Urs von Balthasar, *Kennt uns Jesus – kennen wir ihn* (Freiburg-im-Breisgau: Verlag Herder, 1980); and John Macquarrie, *The Humility of God: Christian Meditations* (London: SCM Press, 1978).
40 On the theme of solidarity and mutuality, cf. A. Vanhoye, *Our Priest is Christ* (Roma: PIB, 1977).

that understands reflection on Jesus in the post-resurrection community as not merely the product and legitimate development of Christian hindsight, but a proper and natural development of what was true of Jesus himself and the impact he made.

In the light of implicit Christology and its claim for delineating the original experience and self-interpretation of Jesus in the language and structure of the New Testament, we can more positively assess the methodology of Balthasar in uncovering the Christological depth of priesthood. Rather than perceiving the language of priesthood as somehow intruding into the original unfolding of Christian ministry, we have come to see it as a primal language, which seeks to express an intrinsic dimension of the 'Form of Christ' unfolding in the whole of Christian experience.

The whole Gospel relates the passion of Jesus' life, all that lay at the centre of his heart, as love for his Father. Jon Sobrino speaks of this 'passion' as the fundamental dynamic of the preaching of the Kingdom, that in its radical praxis was grounded in this most profound interiority of love.[41] And it is here in the interdependence of praxis and interiority that Balthasar's hermeneutics of twofold transcendence with its centre in the humanity of Christ, and the mysteries of his historical life, provide a sound basis for the development of a Christ-centred spirituality of priesthood.[42]

INTEGRATION AND SYNTHESIS

In its radical grasp of the most profound levels of Catholic ecclesial consciousness, Balthasar's methodology is able to uncover what lies at the very heart of what the Church understands about its priesthood. The methodology is not simply a matter of theological speculation nor of the offering of an ideal and beautiful theological synthesis. Rather, it provides a firm underpinning for that correspondence between ecclesial office and personal spiritual identity which *Presbyterorum Ordinis* sets forth as essential for an authentic contemporary spirituality of priesthood when it affirms that each priest represents the Person of Christ himself, being also enriched with special graces. By his serving

---

41 Jon Sobrino, *Christology at the Crossroads* (London: SCM Press, 1978).
42 On Balthasar's emphasis on the inwardness and weight of Christian solidarity, cf. Donald Mackinnon, 'Some Reflections on Balthasar's Christology, with Special Reference to *Theodramatik. II/2 and III*' in *The Analogy of Beauty*, ed. John Riches (Edinburgh: T. and T. Clark, 1986).

the people entrusted to him, he most properly imitates the perfection of the Person of Christ in whose stead he stands.

Sustaining a spirituality that integrates these twin dimensions of priestly existence requires a firm grounding in an Ecclesiology that is Christ-centred. In Balthasar's view, it is clear from the very 'Form' and data of Christian faith, that the personal dimension of priestly existence unfolds precisely from the most profound sense of ecclesial identity, and that the priesthood as a crystallisation of the love of Christ for his Church requires an interiorising that lives out this high ideal of ecclesial identity.[43]

According to some commentators, this sense of interiority is an unnecessary intensification of what is fundamentally a 'task' of service, a view given wide acknowledgement through the writings of Schillebeeckx who would maintain that an undue emphasis on a personal 'priestly' spirituality leads to a 'sacral' model of priesthood that is no longer an appropriate response to the 'signs of the times'. The solidarity with others that the Gospel demands of Christian involvement is in some sense hampered by any language that suggests particularity to this one function among others, albeit significant, in the ambit of Christian ministry.[44]

In the light of Balthasar's hermeneutics of twofold transcendence and its consonance with the language of priesthood in the New Testament as one of twin solidarity, we can meet the objection to 'sacral' language of priesthood by recovering its original and distinctive New Testament meaning in relation to what, in Jesus' life and ministry, had come to be called 'priestly'. In trying to maintain the ecclesial function of the ordained ministry, writers such as Schillebeeckx are attempting to safeguard a valid truth for Christian tradition. They tend, however, to stop short and fail to follow through to the Christological principle that presupposes the ordained ministry, principles that have nothing to do with the establishment of a caste or status, but which exist to make transparent the solidarity between God and us for the sake of whom the Christian priesthood exists.

The 'weight' of this solidarity is such that a merely functional living out of meaning would fail to keep in sight its fundamental characteristic as love. Only an objective and absolute offer of love, greater than the

---

43 For a clear elucidation of Balthasar's view of the synthesis between personal and ecclesial holiness, cf. Antonia Sicari, 'Theology and Holiness', *Communio*, XVI (1989), pp. 351–365.

44 Representative of this view of the function of ministry is Joseph Martos, *Doors to the Sacred* (London: SCM Press, 1981).

human response, transcending any task, can make sense of its presence still in the Church.[45]

Not only does Balthasar's methodology allow for this centring on the 'Christ-Form' at the level of theological reflection, but it provides a horizon for personal spiritual appropriation that leads to a more profound engagement with the world in the light always of that solidarity which Christian faith conceives to be at the heart of the Gospel.

In an illuminating comparison between the theology of Balthasar and certain aspects of liberation theology, Paul E. Ritt points to parallels which have relevance for our study of the dynamic of priestly praxis, and which bring into clearer perspective the need for interiority in the praxis of Christian involvement with the world.[46]

According to Ritt, the theology of liberation with its emphasis on the praxis that unfolds for the preaching of the Kingdom is grounded in the theology of the Cross, which has at its centre the self-giving of Jesus. What Balthasar has to offer to this praxis of the Gospel is an interiority, a mystical dimension that allows for an unforced interrelation between the prayer and social praxis, faith perception of Jesus' Lordship and social activity consistent with the realisation of the Kingdom.

And it is in the synthesis between the conversion of heart and transformation of social structures that Ritt believes Balthasar's Christological method has a unique contribution to make. The affirmation, then, of the primacy of the Form of Christ in ecclesial ministry challenges priesthood to the concrete involvement that manifests Christ's love and changes the world.[47]

For Balthasar, involvement with the world entails a spirituality that is rooted in the specific vision of solidarity that is not only Incarnational but Trinitarian. 'The Christian involvement has its origin in God's involvement . . . it is grounded, captivated by it, shaped and directed by it.'[48] In a Christian community the love we share is a personal act of God Himself in the Person of Christ himself and in its depths contains the interpersonal life of the Trinity; and its breadth enhances

---

45 Thus, in Balthasar's theology, the necessity of a language of the descent of the Trinitarian God of love takes precedence over any notion of the ascent of the religious sensibilities of man.

46 Paul E. Ritt, 'The Lordship of Jesus Christ: Balthasar and Sobrino', *Theological Studies*, 49:4 (December, 1988), pp. 709–731.

47 Ibid., pp. 714–716.

48 Hans Urs von Balthasar, *In Gottes Einsatz leben* (= *Kriterien* 24); 2nd ed. 1972. ET *Engagement with God*, trans. John Halliburton (London: SPCK, 1975), p. 67.

the love of God for the whole world. It is the Trinitarian distinctiveness of Christian solidarity that allows its ministry to meet and love the world in a way that more functional models of engagement cannot envisage. This has to do essentially with the boundlessness of the love of Christ, which the Cross discloses to be the endeavour and expense of the love of the Trinity for the sake of the world.[49]

It is crucial for the interpretation of ministerial priesthood that it has as its measure and meaning no less than the full horizon of Trinitarian involvement. Seeing priesthood in the light of the mystery of Christ requires that the characteristics of life which the mystery reveals must not be lost sight of when attempting to describe the characteristics of Christ's Priesthood in the Church and world of today.[50]

49 Cf. W.H. Vanstone, *Love's Endeavour, Love's Expense: The Response of Being in the Love of God* (London: Darton, Longman and Todd, 1977).
50 See also the works of Avery Dulles on the representation of Christ in the ministerial priesthood and his seminal thinking on this in 'Models for Ministerial Priesthood', *Origins*, 20 (1990), pp. 284–89. See also E. J. Kilmartin, 'Apostolic Office: Sacrament of Christ', *Theological Studies*, 36 (1975), p. 261.

II

JESUS: PRIEST AND VICTIM

THE DEEPER CHRISTOLOGICAL SETTING

A THEOLOGY OF THE CROSS

According to Balthasar, it is the theology of the Cross that unlocks the mystery of Jesus' identity as Priest, for here the figure of the obedient Son appears as the most definitive representation of the Triune love of God. God is Himself eternal, loving, self-emptying and groundlessly free. He reveals Himself in the self-giving obedience of the Son on the Cross. The obedience of Jesus is an obedience of total co-operation with sinners, representing the totally unique transference of his eternal love as the Son towards the ever greater Father.

For Balthasar it is the theological concern of the obedient love of the Son in its Trinitarian depths that most clearly illumines the mystery of Christ and his redemptive mission, and it is this that constitutes his theology of the Priesthood of Christ.

It is a theological concept that gathers together the most profound themes of Christology, i.e. the kenosis of the Son, the surrender of the Son, substitution, love and expiation, God-forsakenness and abandonment, and glorification and resurrection. These themes are not treated separately, one after the other, but are integrated into a Christological 'moment' that discloses the whole thread running through the life of Jesus from his Incarnation in Mary to his death on the Cross as the drama of Trinitarian love for the world unfolding in the mission-sending of the Son.[1]

All Balthasar's thinking strives towards this 'Theodramatic of the

---

1 Balthasar's main soteriology which is always centred on the theology of the Cross is contained in his seminal essay, 'Mysterium Paschale', in J. Feiner and M. Lohrer, ed., *Mysterium Salutis, Vol. III/2* (Einsiedeln: Benziger, 1969); ET *Mysterium Paschale*, trans. Aiden Nichols, OP (Edinburgh: T. and T. Clark, 1990). These seminal insights are developed thematically in *Theodramatik*, particularly in *Vol. II/2: Die Personen in Christus* and *Vol. III: Die Handlung* (Einsiedeln: Johannes Verlag, 1978, 1980). Cf. also, for a review of Balthasar's achievement, John O'Donnell, 'The Trinity in Recent German Theology', *Heythrop Journal*, 123: (1982), pp. 115–167.

Cross', and in all theological questions he seeks to explore the ramifications of this definitive Form of divine self-giving love, that while shattering all human forms of love and service, at the same time becomes the ground of a new and radical experience of what Christian *agape* is called to become. In the context of ministerial priesthood, this more clearly delineates the distinctive 'form' of pastoral love to which priests are called to witness in their pastoral vocation. Furthermore, this 'form' discloses what is at stake in preaching the Gospel of Christ in terms of allowing what we think and say of Christian faith to do some little justice to the unique and unsurpassable drama of Triune love for the world that grounds and directs Christian involvement, as always for the sake of that greater love.

Finally in holding on to a language of theology that continues to speak of Christ as Priest and Victim, we are brought face to face with what we see only in a mirror dimly, the glimpse of the Christian mystery of God who, without leaving His own side, comes over to ours. This crossing over towards humankind and the surrender of all the richness of divine love into our hands takes on the Form of the Son who, allowing himself to be delivered over by the Father to sinners, 'lays bare the heart of the Father' and the extent of His love for the world.

Only in His holding on to nothing for himself is God Father of all: He pours forth his substance and generates the Son, and only in the holding on to nothing for himself of what has been received does the Son show himself to be of the same essence of the Father. In the shared holding on to nothing are they one in the Spirit, who is the personification of this eternal product of this ceaselessly flowing movement of love. If one of these Persons steps out of the encircling life in order to offer the world the totality of God, his style of life will not be the grasping demeanour of a Pantocrator, but the opposite. The Son lays bare the heart of the Father as he becomes the servant of all and breathes into the world his Spirit of service and of taking the last place.[2]

Such a vision keeps the total shape of Christian revelation alive for Christian interpretation and praxis. In the context of ministerial priesthood we shall ask whether such a vision still has a function in interpreting Christian priestly identity. In a theological climate that tends to question the continuing validity and relevance of concepts

---

2 Hans Urs von Balthasar, *Pneuma und Institution* (= *Skizzen zur Theologie IV*) (Einsiedeln: Johannes Verlag, 1974). For Balthasar the drama between God and the world is made possible only by the primordial drama of the eternal Trinity, in which the separation between the Father and Son is bridged in eternity by the Holy Spirit.

such as priest, victim, expiation or substitution, any continuation of
this classical theological imagery must be defended on the grounds of
its theological consistency with the data of Christian revelation. If it
can be shown to be consistent, then the onus is on theological models
that have abandoned this theological category, to defend the apparent
absence of a dimension of Christian reality that bears the crisis of the
Cross as an enduring hermeneutic for Christian involvement in the
world.

As we attempt to explore Balthasar's own unique demonstration of
this hermeneutic, we shall attempt to place his work within the context
of other theologians who seek also to engage in a theology of the Cross,[3]
as well as delineating its more precise horizon for an interpretation of
the identity of Christian priesthood that can never, in Balthasar's view,
lose sight of the absolute character of crucified love. If it is to glimpse
its own truth and identity in the light of the mystery of Christ – his
love for the Father and for the Father's sake – his love for the world,
priesthood requires constant reference to an underlying theology of the
Cross.

We shall begin by distilling from Balthasar's most explicit treatment
of the doctrine of Christian priesthood, to be found in *Christlicher
Stand*,[4] the main features of the theology of priesthood, both in its
relation to the Person of Christ and in its continuation in the Church.
Having identified the features, we shall explore each of them under
their deepest, most distinctive Christological settings, the first to do
with the obedience of the Son to his mission, the second in the light
of the kenosis of the Son, which is to characterise his mission and is
the key to unlocking his priestly identity.

In the second half of the chapter we shall move into what Balthasar
sees as the heart of the drama of the kenosis of the Son, which is the
double surrender of the Father and Son in their love for the world.
Here we outline his highly original use of the theological categories
of expiation and substitution which lead us into a critical understanding

---

3 For a comprehensive treatment of contemporary theologies of the Cross, which
includes those of Balthasar, Rahner, Moltmann, Schillebeeckx and Sobrino, cf. Anne
Murphy, SHCJ, 'Contemporary Theologies of the Cross', *The Way*, 28 (1988), pp.
149–163. Also cf., James Alison, *Knowing Jesus* (London: SPCK, 1993), who explores
the ideas of R. Gerard on the imaginative power of the meaning of redemption; and
of R. Schwager's reflection on the persistence of the image of the victim and scapegoat
in Christian tradition.
4 Hans Urs von Balthasar, *Christlicher Stand* (Einsiedeln: Johannes Verlag, 1977); ET
The Christian State of Life, trans. Sr Mary Frances McCarthy (San Francisco: Ignatius
Press, 1983).

of what is meant by continuing to speak of Jesus as both Priest and Victim.

Finally we shall assess the validity of this language for Christian priesthood and seek to demonstrate its power still to touch Christian experience and to share both ecclesial and priestly self-understanding.

PRIESTHOOD – CHRIST'S STATE OF LIFE

In *Christlicher Stand* Balthasar describes in some detail what he conceives to constitute the Priesthood of Christ. In the first place he identifies priesthood with Christ's state of life which is characterised by 'the stand he takes in the loving will of the Father through the perfect gift of all that is his to the Father, and for the Father's sake to the world.'[5] He then proceeds to speak of this stance in terms of a surrender, which acquires the inner form of sacrifice.

> In his mission of reconciliation and mediation, Christ invests the gift of himself to the Father and the Father's acceptance of it with the modality that makes it the emptying of all that he is . . . when the Son stands before the Father in readiness to give himself . . . he thus abandons to the Father the disposal of what is his . . . he becomes potentially a victim to be sacrificed.[6]

According to Balthasar this potential of Christ to both offer himself and of himself being offered, to be himself both Priest and Victim, is not simply realised in the Gethsemane and Golgotha experiences, but is at the heart of the mystery of the Incarnation, '. . . when the Son divests himself of his likeness to God to enter upon the state of one who is both the Priest who offers and the Victim who is offered.'[7] The efficacy of this sacrifice depends entirely on the inner disposition of love, the inner modalities of the Son's perfect love which Balthasar believes cannot fail to signify the establishment of his Priesthood.

Jesus is the definitive Priest precisely because, in the very act of offering the sacrificial victim, he becomes himself the Victim that is offered.

Balthasar maintains that priesthood is not simply an image that accrues to Jesus, but is intrinsic to his very nature, having its source in the very essence of his own divine Person. This is because it is the

5 Ibid., p. 252.
6 Ibid.
7 Ibid., p. 255.

mode of his gift of himself to the Father and is an expression of his consecration:

> He is consecrated priest, *par excellence*, by his very nature ... he contains in himself the concept of all that is priestly ... containing in himself the unity of priestly office and love.[8]

It is his unbounded readiness to give himself to the Father for our sake, *pro nobis*, that allows him to supplant and transcend the official priesthood of the Old Covenant, in which function sought to be identified with person and action, and in consequence to become one with passion. In Jesus these come together, especially on the Cross, where the priestly function reaches its climax and where office is seen to be no longer visible. On the Cross we have only the victim and the death of obediential love that supersedes all legal and external blood offerings.

From here on Balthasar takes us more deeply into the experience and life-form of Jesus as Priest when he speaks of the act of sacrifice acquiring, in the light of the Cross, the characteristics of pure objectivity, the characteristics of an official priesthood.

According to Balthasar, it is the limitless nature of the divine self-giving that makes it absolute, so much so, that even the awareness of love can be sacrificed for the sake of love. This is what happens on the Cross, when the Father Himself, who conceals His love in the darkness of the night for the sake of the redemption, appears in the pure objectivity and absolute impartiality of the priesthood. Balthasar describes such a priesthood as the mode in which love itself achieves its ultimate gift – the sacrifice of itself.

> The naked formality of crucified love is the great proof of Trinitarian love for the world, and herein lies the heart of the priesthood. It is for this reason that the infinite love between Father and Son assumes on the Cross the modality of pure obedience and hence of official priesthood ... in this way signifying both the complete obscuring of their mutual love and the complete revelation of its boundlessness.[9]

According to Balthasar, this characteristic of love can never be lost sight of in the mystery of Christian and ecclesial living. Objective office therefore exists to guarantee and sustain the dynamic of self-given love as a source from which the Church must never withdraw.

8 Ibid., p. 252.
9 Ibid., p. 253.

In his treatment of the image of priesthood in relation to Christ, Balthasar obviously reaches an intensity in his imaginative use of theological concepts that of themselves may not always appear so compelling. The language of passivity, of the one who in his readiness to let himself be given and thus suffers the eclipse of love, is a language that requires closer examination if it is to yield its most profound Christological and ecclesial meaning.

This can only happen if we more guardedly unpack the Christological presuppositions behind his creative and intense language and imagery. If some have seen in this a weakness in Balthasar's method,[10] there can also be found a strength in that he risks in his theological endeavour to find appropriate language to give expression to the most profound realities of Christian faith, i.e. the involvement of God for the sake of the world, in the very darkness and imagery in which the world has lost its way.

That God Himself has opened up a way for us through the very experiences of sin and death which otherwise would separate us from Him is for Balthasar the access to God that comes about in the liturgy of Jesus' life, passion and death. This language of passion and death is ultimately a translation of the language of resurrected love. The soteriological 'for us' of the Cross is grounded in the unbounded victory of Trinitarian love overcoming our refusal of its offer of love. The Priesthood of Christ is the free obedience of the Son to accept his mission of making the fact of our refusal and separation paradoxically the way to the most intimate and intense union of love between God and ourselves.

THE OBEDIENCE OF THE SON TO HIS MISSION

THE MISSION OF THE SON

Mission, or 'sending' (*Sendung*), is a principal *leitmotif* in Balthasar's Christology and in particular of his theological trilogy, *Theodramatik*, which explores the whole of revelation as a divine drama. This is apparent in the New Testament witness, where Jesus is the eternal Son sent into the world by the Father, a strongly Johannine theme,

---

10 Cf. J. Kay, 'Hans Urs von Balthasar: Post-Critical Theologian', *Concilium* 14: 84–89 (1981); also J.N. Faux, 'Un Théologien: Hans Urs von Balthasar', *Nouvelle Revue Théologique*, 94 (1972), pp. 1009–1030.

but not exclusively so. It is found also in the Synoptic tradition and in the teaching of St Paul. Balthasar underlines John's mission-Christology as simply the logical unpacking of what is already implied in the Synoptics which testify to Jesus' unique awareness of being sent. John O'Donnell points out:

> Balthasar reveals his preference for the Fourth Gospel according to St. John . . . Time and time again Balthasar returns to such Johanine texts as 4:34: 'My food is to do the will of him who sent me and to accomplish his work'; and 6:38: 'I have come down from heaven, not to do my will, but the will of him who sent me'; and 8:29: 'I do always the things that please him'. Here we see the centre of Jesus' existence in his obedience. So much is this the case that Balthasar says that Jesus' 'where' is in the Father. He writes: 'The Son's "where" which fixes his state, is always clear, regardless of whether he is in the bosom of the Father, or on the stage of the world; it is the mission, the task, the will of the Father.'[11]

Balthasar is indebted here to St Thomas' exposition of the divine mission, in which the temporal mission of the Son and the Spirit presupposes and manifests the eternal procession from which Balthasar concludes that in Jesus, Person and mission are identical. He is the 'sent' Son; his mission is indivisibly contained within his priesthood.[12]

This concept of mission integrates not only Christology and Trinity, but all the mysteries of Christ's life. Together they constitute his mission.

According to Balthasar, the experiential dimension at the heart of the theological concept of mission is the obedient love of the Son, which of course is essentially a New Testament constituent of what is priestly about Jesus. This sense of a primordial obedience within the meaning and thread of Jesus' life runs very deep in Balthasar's reflection. At the beginning of all his work there is found obedience: the readiness to let himself be disposed of by the Father according to his total will. The path from the heart of the eternal Father to the womb of Mary, his mother, is already an experience of the way of obedience for Jesus who is always radically open to the Father's will.

This obedience to his mission is the origin of Jesus' preaching of

---

11 John O'Donnell, 'Hans Urs von Balthasar: The Form of His Theology', *Communio*, XVI (1989), pp. 461ff.
12 For a clear exposition of the Thomistic background to Balthasar's Christology, cf. John Saward, *The Mysteries of March* (London: Collins, 1990), pp. 11–17 and 55–88.

the Kingdom and of his actions which signify its immanence. It is for the sake of the Father's love that Jesus gives himself unconditionally to his mission, and it is this quality of unconditional self-giving that Balthasar identifies with the inner disposition of love that makes Jesus' life an existential gift of self, a true sacrifice.

Obedience becomes, then, the mode of self-giving love; not an extrinsic following out of a mission, but the deepest coming into one's own being as person through the embrace of one's mission. In Balthasar's perception of the unity of Person and mission in Jesus, the intra-personal relation of Triune love is clearly evoked: Jesus is the sent Son, his obedience is directed to the Father who sends, and it is lived out in the Holy Spirit.

> In Christ, therefore, penetrating the whole doomed predicament of human existence and being obedient to the Father's directions are simply one and the same . . . All norms, ultimately, come down to the Son's unlimited capacity for obedience: the Father asks him to give tangible proof of the divine love for the world and loads upon him the totality of men's free turning away from God.[13]

This picture of primordial obedience is not conceived of as subservience or domination, but is grounded in the filial way in which the Son possesses the one divine will with the Father and the Spirit. For Balthasar the obedience of Christ is the revelation in human form of the eternal love of the divine Son for his eternal Father, who has eternally begotten him out of love; it is the theological crystallisation of the Johannine insight/tradition in which Jesus says in the Farewell Discourse: 'I do as the Father has commanded me, so that the world may know that I love the Father' (Jn 14:31).

Christ's obedience, then, is both the exegesis of the Trinity's life and love and the most definite access in life to the inner disposition of the love of that incomparable and unique human life. In biblical terms this has to do with having 'that mind which was in Christ Jesus' (Phil. 2:5), namely, engaging with the very heart of the biblical witness to the meaning of the Passion and Cross of Christ, whose solidarity, and therefore whose Priesthood, involved 'becoming as all men are, even to accepting death, death on a cross' (Phil. 2:8). Obedience to his mission led Jesus to embrace his Priestly identity, an identity that

13 Hans Urs von Balthasar, *Theodramatik, vol. II/1: Der Mensch in Gott* (Einsiedeln: Johannes Verlag, 1976); ET *Theodrama: Man in God*, trans. Graham Harrison (San Francisco: Ignatius Press, 1990).

Balthasar shows to be fully disclosed in the Mystery of the self-emptying love of the Son.

KENOSIS: THE FORM OF THE SELF-GIVING OF THE SON

According to Balthasar, the theological 'function' of the kenosis is to establish that what is enabled in the Incarnation is not merely the Son assuming creatureliness in general, but the assumption of the concrete human destiny that stands under the 'curse' of sin and death. In the light of the kenosis we come to see that the Incarnation has no other ultimate purpose than the Cross.

For Balthasar it is because Jesus is the unique bearer of the world's sin and, because the source of this identity is his unique relation to the Father, that the concept of kenosis is central and definitive for Christian theology.[14] The human obedience of the Son presupposes a divine decision taken in advance, implying the surrender of the *Forma Dei*. As Balthasar observes, this requires that theology must consider:

> . . . how such a surrender can be possible for the God of whom we cannot postulate any alteration as this is found in creatures, nor any suffering and obeying in the manner of creatures.[15]

Balthasar finds the solution of this problem in relating kenosis to the Doctrine of God, positing an incomprehensible freedom in God that allows Him to do otherwise and to be other than the creature would suppose of Him on the grounds of its concept of God.

Balthasar's treatment of the concept of kenosis has been the subject of considerable scrutiny and comment across the broad spectrum of theological traditions. Donald MacKinnon, in his reflection on the Christology of the Theodramatic,[16] points out that in his presentation of the relationship of the Trinity to the Cross, Balthasar shows himself to be fully attentive to the idea that proper understanding of the crucifixion and resurrection requires their treatment of the Doctrine of God Himself. In this perspective kenosis is actually *plerosus*, which means that the human self-emptying limitations of Jesus are seen to

14 For a consideration of the persistence of the kenosis in Christian theology, cf. S.W. Sykes, 'The Strange Persistence of Kenotic Christology', in *Being and Truth: Essays in Honour of John Macquarrie*, ed. Alistair Kee and Eugene Thomas Long (London: SCM Press, 1986).
15 Hans Urs von Balthasar, *Mysterium Paschale*, p. 24.
16 Donald Mackinnon, 'Some Reflections on Hans Urs von Balthasar's Christology', in *The Analogy of Beauty* (Edinburgh: T&T Clark, 1986), pp. 164–174.

be a positive expression of his divinity rather than a curtailment of it.[17]

It is at this level of interpretation that Balthasar probes the kenotic dimension of the Christian Doctrine of God, in which Christ's obedience, even unto the Cross, is perceived as the form which he gives to his love of the Father. Kenosis is the most perfect expression of the eternal life of love within the Trinity; it is not a diminishment in God, does no violence to the Godhead, and is at one and the same time both the 'doxa' and 'drama' of divine involvement in and for the world, for whom the Son is given.[18]

Here Balthasar recognises theological precedent for the task and cites in particular the reflection of Hilary on the power of the divine Son to make himself powerless. But he moves away from what he calls a focus on the 'divine nature' into the Trinitarian context of the personal relationships in God.[19]

This way of approaching a theology of kenosis sets Balthasar apart from other 'kenotic' theologians who attempt to resolve the apparent contradictions directly in holding on to the twin polarities of Christology: The immutability of the Divine Nature and the suffering and death of the man, Jesus. G.F. O'Hanlon, in his study of Balthasar's treatment of the theme of the immutability of God, affirms that constant restraint is the most appropriate response to this mystery of faith.[20] Authentic Christology does not attempt to explain the mystery away, but enters more deeply into its meaning and function for Christian living. It is clear that Balthasar remains sensitive to this crucial principle of Christological enquiry.

By keeping his reflection on kenosis within the strict boundaries of the Trinitarian context, Balthasar maintains the integrity of his theological task, and at the same time he surrenders to the persistence of kenosis in Christian reality by attempting to face squarely its challenge to theology.

---

17 In his preface to *Mysterium Paschale*, Balthasar points out that kenosis is not a self-emptying in the form of a renunciation of the nature of God Himself, but is the most perfect expression of the eternal event of the divine processions of love; cf. *Mysterium Paschale*, p. viii.

18 Ibid., p. 82.

19 Ibid., p. 29.

20 Cf. G.F. O'Hanlon, SJ, *The Immutability of God in the Theology of Hans Urs von Balthasar* (Cambridge: The University Press, 1990), in which O'Hanlon argues for a positive assessment of Balthasar's overall attempt at keeping a delicate balance in the interrelationships between the witness of Scripture, tradition, Christian experience, the logic and dynamics of philosophical systems and his own presuppositions and biases in the treatment of the complex issues of Christology, pp. 174ff.

For Balthasar the self-giving of Jesus and indeed his very death is the perfect expression of the eternal willingness of Father and Son to be love for each other and for the world. As John Saward so appropriately summarises:

> This then is Trinitarian Kenosis: God in himself is a consubstantial communion of selfless, self-emptied persons. In a word, God is love; Triune love. He does not lose anything in the dance of dispossession. In the Trinity, having and giving away are one.[21]

According to Balthasar, therefore, the analogical kenosis of the divine relations is what makes possible all the other *kenoses*: in creation, covenant and redemptive Incarnation. The Incarnational kenosis is a work both of divine freedom and divine omnipotence. 'God's almighty power "blazes forth",' says Balthasar, 'in the powerlessness of the Incarnate and Crucified Son.'[22]

In *Mysterium Paschale*, Balthasar presents a powerful and beautiful account of what kenosis in this Trinitarian context discloses about the wonder and mystery of the divine involvement. In the first place, kenosis relates to God and His self-giving in creation. It is the selflessness within the Godhead that is the basis of the first form of kenosis that lies in creation, for the Creator gives up a part of His freedom to the creature in the act of creating. But this He can dare to do only in virtue of foreseeing and taking into account the second and truer kenosis, that of the Cross, in which He makes good the uttermost consequences of creation and freedom and goes beyond them.[23]

In this kenosis, the surrender of the Form of God becomes the definitive translation of the love of the Son who gives expression to his being of the Father and his total dependence on Him in the form of obedient love. The whole of the Trinity is involved in this act: 'The Father by sending out the Son, and abandoning him on the Cross, and the Spirit by uniting them now only in the expressive form of the separation.'[24]

Thus Balthasar finds no contradiction between the self-giving and abandonment of the Son and his own essence. Rather, there is a complete correspondence between his divine essence and his

---

21 John Saward, *The Mysteries of March*, p. 29.

22 Hans Urs von Balthasar, *Mysterium Paschale*, p. 35.

23 Here Balthasar is seen to be indebted to Maximus the Confessor; cf. *Mysterium Paschale*, pp. 21, 38, and 78.

24 Ibid. p. 35, where Balthasar explores the parallels of his Trinitarian understanding of kenosis with that of the Orthodox theologian Bulgakov.

self-emptying love. According to Balthasar there is no necessity or intrinsic demand of the structure of creation that would lead to the deduction of this decision of grace that led to kenosis. In *Love Alone; the Way of Revelation*,[25] this radical dimension of the Christian mystery of faith as the 'several mysteries' which one has to believe, are simply aspects of the love we receive in Christ. The Father is the sender who sends in order that the obedient (kenotic) character of the Son's love may never be lost to sight. The Spirit is the one breathed forth to reveal the freedom and fruitfulness of a love beyond understanding, and to reveal the inwardness, the testifying power, the glory and pure autonomy conferred by that love.

The fact that the horizon of the love given to us always greatly exceeds our own, and that the disparity can never be wiped away, provides the stimulus for deepening our understanding of kenosis in Christian theology and its consequences for Christian praxis.

Balthasar's creative treatment of the concept of kenosis is one that interpenetrates with the most profound themes of New Testament Christology. In Balthasar, even as it reaches lyrical intensity, his fundamental position remains true to the fundamental structure of the New Testament witness. By unravelling the doctrinal presuppositions of kenosis in the New Testament, Balthasar shows it to be an unforced development of the dimension of unconditional love that characterised Jesus' existence and ultimately led him to rejection and death. As so many scholars affirm, the historical situation of Jesus' ministry and death contained within it the elements that would ultimately have to lead to his rejection and death.[26] In particular his teaching on and offering to sinners of the gift of forgiveness and the areas in which he 'broke boundaries' that were considered sacrosanct between man and God, support rather than undermine Balthasar's more panoramic theological explanation of the self-giving life and ministry of Jesus.

According to Balthasar, the unfolding of the Theodrama of kenosis in Jesus' life is a Form hidden within the stylised forms and traditions of the Gospels. In *Herrlichkeit, III*, Balthasar identifies the glory and

25 Hans Urs von Balthasar, *Glaubhaft ist nur Liebe* (= *Christ heute* V/1) (Einsiedeln: Johannes Verlag, 1966); ET *Love Alone: The Way of Revelation*, trans. Alexander Dru (New York: Herder and Herder, 1969).
26 For an excellent study of the redemptive and sacrificial dimensions of the earliest Christian tradition, cf., *Sacrifice and Redemption: Durham Essays in Theology*, ed. S.W. Sykes (Cambridge: The University Press, 1991); Gerald O'Collins, *The Calvary Christ* (London: SCM Press, 1977); Jürgen Moltmann, *The Crucified God* (London: SCM Press, 1974); and Martin Hengel, *The Cross of the Son of God* (London: SCM Press, 1986).

aesthetic of divine love with the unfolding of Jesus' own life and ministry. Thus the evangelists' task was to make clear the essential hiddenness of both 'Theodrama' and 'Doxa' in Jesus' inner experience and public life.

It is particularly in his self-donation to 'those who were his own in the world'[27] that we glimpse the initial gestures of a self-emptying love that is ultimately to be given to a world that does not know how to love in return. In the disciples' failure to respond equally to the love that is given, they become the witness to the lengths and 'precipice' of love,[28] beyond which they cannot go; the place where only Jesus can be, the place of Golgotha, where the love of Father and Son is given definitively for the sake of all.

What kenosis discloses about the boundlessness of the divine love is its complete identity with the vulnerable humanity of Jesus.

Kenosis has direct consequences for the interpretation of Christian priesthood which is conceived to be fundamentally a life of service. What is distinctive about Christian 'service' and love cannot be fully revealed without a reliance on what was from the very beginning considered to be its paradigm and inspiration. And this, we are told by Scripture, is not merely praxis, but 'a state of mind', an interiorisation of the mind of Christ, his stance towards the Father and towards us:

Though he was in the form of God,
Jesus did not count equality with God a thing to be grasped.

He emptied himself,
taking the form of a servant,
being born in the likeness of men.

And being found in human form,
he humbled himself and became obedient unto death,
even death on a cross.
Therefore God has highly exalted him
and bestowed on him the name which is above every name,

That at the name of Jesus every knee should bow,
in heaven and on earth and under the earth,

---

27 A gesture of self-donation that remains at the heart of Christian liturgy and prayer. Cf. 'Eucharistic Prayer IV'.

28 A constant theme in Balthasar's thought, cf. *Glaubhaft ist nur Liebe*, pp. 87ff.

And every tongue confess that Jesus Christ is Lord,
to the glory of God the Father.

(Phil. 2:6–11)

THE SURRENDER OF THE SON

Balthasar both deepens and develops the theology of the Cross with
its dimensions of self-giving love and kenosis, in his confrontation
with what he believes to be at the heart of the Christological witness
of the New Testament, i.e. the doctrine of expiation and substitution.
Commenting on this emphasis which is found throughout Balthasar's
entire Christological endeavours, John Saward writes:

> According to the New Testament, and the Nicene Creed, the Son
> of God became man, died and rose again 'for us' (*hyper hemon, pro
> nobis*). For Balthasar these two little words are the first and most
> fundamental words of the Christian Faith, but he feels that certain
> interpretations of them fall seriously short of their full meaning. *Pro
> nobis* means, for example, much more than for the benefit of, more
> than in solidarity with . . . Balthasar claims that when the Church
> confesses that the Incarnate Son suffered and died 'for us' she means
> he changed places with us. Our costly redemption was a work of
> substitution.[29]

The clearest witness in the New Testament to this doctrine is in
the writings of St Paul. It is Paul who develops and theologically works
out the full consequences of the Passion and Cross as a Trinitarian
event. The key concept used in the Pauline testimony is the word
paradidomi, which means 'delivering up' or 'handing over'. Together
with other contemporary theologians, Balthasar insists that the full
implications of the *paradidomi* must not be diminished or watered
down because it expresses, as no other word can, the distinctive
Christian nuance of what the giving and sending of the Son meant in
a Trinitarian context.[30] According to Balthasar, that handing over of
the Son manifests Trinitarian love. The Father loves the world so much

---

29 John Saward, *The Mysteries of March*, p. 39.
30 Cf. Hans Urs von Balthasar, *Theodramatik, vol. III*, and *Herrlichkeit, vol. II/1:
Klerikale Stile* (Einsiedeln: Johannes Verlag, 1962), in which Balthasar elucidates the
classical doctrine of atonement in the light of Anselm and of the originating form of
Trinitarian self-giving love.

that He does not spare His only Son, but gives him up for the sake of all (cf. Jn 3:16; Rom. 8:32). In bringing out the Trinitarian depths to this vital theme of the New Testament, Balthasar gives expression, not only to the historical sense of handing over of the Lord in his self-emptied weakness from the inaugurating moment with Judas to the final moment of death, but also to the whole series of 'handings over': to the Temple police, the chief priests and Sanhedrin, the Roman authority and Pontius Pilate, the soldiers and Herod, the crowd, and finally into the depths of Trinitarian selflessness which is manifested in Christ's human relation. Christ wants to put himself where men are in their misery, not just statically alongside them, but dynamically, in revelation of the intra-Trinitarian ecstasy of love, taking over their burden from them, which is a suffering not just *like theirs*, but in their place or stead.[31]

The objection that is often raised against the concept of the 'handing over' of the Son has to do not with the depth of love that is expressed in the New Testament images and language of redemption, but with the specific image of the Father as somehow an 'executioner', delivering up the Son out of a brutal sense of justice. Gerald O'Collins, in his critique of Balthasar's theology of expiation, views the language of substitution as Balthasar handles it as a distortion of the New Testament perception of redemptive love. It also fails, he asserts, to engage with the reality of resurrected love which overcomes the isolation of sin and death in its victory and a triumph of love.[32] This point of view is taken up also by Schillebeeckx, Mackey and others, who dismiss any possibility of holding on to this imagery in contemporary religious language. For these writers the story of Jesus' passion, death and resurrection is but a protest against suffering and death in which any language of substitution eclipses the power of the Gospel to save.

A closer examination of Balthasar's theology seems to be called for in the face of these critiques, in particular the distinction of Balthasar's interpretation of the 'handing over', which distances him from other theological assertions which tend towards images of the Father's will in the face of annihilation and crucifixion. In *Trinity and Temporality*,

31 The antecedents for this concept run deep within the whole of the sacrificial tradition in the Old Testament, from the Binding of Isaac in Genesis 22, and through to the cult of the Day of Atonement in the Second Temple, at the time of Jesus. Cf., Shalom Spiegel, *The Last Trial* (New York: Schocken Books, 1967); and A.J. Heschel, *God in Search of Man* (New York: Harper and Row, 1955).

32 Cf. Gerald O'Collins, *Jesus Risen* (London: Darton, Longman and Todd, 1987).

John J. O'Donnell, SJ[33] argues that according to Balthasar, it would be a mistake to see the Father's will as an imposition upon the Son, as something alien to him. O'Donnell makes the point that for Balthasar, the delivering up of the Son by the Father can only be interpreted by the fuller Trinitarian development of the double surrender of Father and Son. Balthasar himself says:

> Again we find that this death, which is both freely embraced by him *and* laid on him from outside, presupposes a twofold love: the love of the Father, who lays this burden on him, and the love of the Son who bears it. In the context of this death, there is so much insistence on the Father's love for us that there seems to be no place for the kind of misunderstanding (for example, of the Anselmian teaching) according to which the Father is thought to be concerned solely for his honor and surrenders his Son on that account. It all goes back once more to the loving decision made by the Trinity, in which the Holy Spirit of love is just as involved as the Father and Son, guaranteeing and fulfilling the unanimity of their love in that deadly abandonment of the Cross ... Nothing prevents us from understanding the Son's death in obedience to the Father as a death *for love* of the Father, for the implementation of his will to the uttermost. In the end, therefore, it is the human expression of a shared love-death in a supereminently trinitarian sense: the One who forsakes is just as much affected (in his eternal life) as the One who is forsaken, and just as much as the forsaking and forsaken love that is One in the Holy Spirit.[34]

In this light, the joint action of Father and Son is not a decree of execution, but the Father's willingness to suffer the loss of the Son and the Son's readiness to lay down his life for the sake of the Father's love for all.

Balthasar explores this 'double surrender' in his sustained reflection on the themes of the Paschal mystery, *Mysterium Paschale*.[35] Balthasar shows that we come to the heart of the mystery of the Cross. Only when we perceive it as an event between the Father and the Son, a twofold surrender in love towards the world that involves the whole Trinity, do we overcome any perceived opposition between a *theologia crucis* and a *theologia gloriae*. Balthasar, quoting Karl Barth, writes:

33 John J. O'Donnell, SJ, *Trinity and Temporality* (Oxford: The University Press, 1983).
34 Cf. Hans Urs von Balthasar, *Theodramatik, vol. III*, p. 501.
35 *Mysterium Paschale*, pp. 136ff.

A *theologia gloriae*, celebrating what Jesus Christ in his Resurrection, received for us, and what he is for us as the Risen One, would have no meaning unless it also contained in itself the *theologia crucis*: the praise of what he has done for us in his death and of what he is for us as the crucified. But no more would an abstract *theologia crucis* have meaning. One cannot celebrate in proper fashion the passion and death of Jesus Christ, if this praise does not already contain in itself the *theologia gloriae*: the praise of him who, in his Resurrection, receives our justice and our life, the One who rose for us from among the dead.[36]

There is for Balthasar a divine recklessness and magnanimity that needs constantly to be brought to the centre of Christian and ecclesial consciousness. It is for this reason that he takes a critical stance towards the ideas of 'solidarity' and 'gift of self' that are deemed theologically viable and sufficient to replace concepts such as 'substitution' and 'ransom'.[37]

Balthasar's insistence on the 'maximilist thesis' that there is a genuine exchange of place in the incarnate and redemptive mission of the Son is a problem in his theology for some. It remains a continuing challenge by stubbornly refusing to eclipse the profound mysteries of self-giving love at the heart of the Christian revelation of God.

JESUS, PRIEST AND VICTIM

Through the prism of Balthasar's opening up of the richness of the theology of the Cross as a drama of love within the life of the Trinity, we have come to the point where we can glimpse more clearly the twin dimensions of Jesus' existence both as one who is passively given up and as one who lets himself be given. Here we encounter a fully articulated language about Jesus as both Priest and Victim: the one who offers; the one who is offered up. In divine freedom he is eternally ready to be given up; in human freedom he actively gives himself up. So he is Lamb and Sacrifice (Jn 1:28) and self-giving Priest (Heb. 3:14). The context and words of institution at the Last Supper show that his self-giving precedes any 'giving up' by the hand of others. Balthasar writes:

36 Karl Barth, *Kirchliche Dogmatik IV/1* (Zurich: Zollikon, 1953), p. 622, quoted in *Mysterium Paschale*, p. 82.
37 Cf. Hans Urs von Balthasar, *Theodramatik, vol. III*, pp. 266–268.

This gift of self is only an act in the sense of being a consent to be delivered. This has to be seen in a Trinitarian context. The whole juridical action is contained within the love of the Father who gives him up and the love of the Son who lets himself be disposed of.[38]

The Incarnate Son's experiences of self-giving in his human nature constitute his Priesthood; the apparent estrangement and absence of the Father in His abandonment of the Son to the dereliction of the Cross is the new and radical liturgy that gives access to God.

The Son takes estrangement on himself and creates nearness, nearness to God as man because of the union of Father and Son maintained in the midst of all the darkness and dereliction. The estrangement and separation from the Father of the Son is the most radical bond of unity between them both; in bearing our sinful distance and transforming it by opening up for us a way through our estrangement with the Father, Jesus constantly lives out his mission, i.e. his Priesthood, in which the otherness of our sin and alienation is therefore replaced by the Trinitarian otherness of love.

In this development of the Priesthood of Christ, Balthasar integrates the notion of Victimhood in a way that wholly corresponds to what we earlier understood to be Vanhoye's exegetical assessment of what priesthood means in relation to Jesus.[39] It expresses a deep conformity to the Synoptic account of the Ministry of Jesus, according to which Jesus' life and preaching is characterised by a complete solidarity with the sinful and lost, which the Gethsemane narrative also records was a transparent response to the will of the Father that Jesus should drink the cup of solidarity in suffering.

As Dillistone has made clear in his monumental work on the doctrine of the Atonement,[40] the original 'atoning' dimension to Jesus' life was precisely in those profound experiences of him and of the Father's compassion, given particularly to the poor and the lost.

In response to those theologians who believe that it is no longer necessary to maintain a language of priesthood and victim for Christian ministry, it is essential to root any continuation of this theological language of vicariousness in its original Gospel setting. While it is authentic to seek other language to do justice to the compassion of God at the heart of the Christian faith, the reality of this compassion

---

38 Hans Urs von Balthasar, *Christlicher Stand*, p. 257.
39 See above, Chapter I.
40 F.W. Dillistone, *The Christian Understanding of Atonement* (London, SCM Press, 1984).

as it unfolds in the drama of Jesus' life and ministry, leading ultimately to death and to God-forsakenness on the Cross, needs be continually kept alive if the founding vision or paradigm is to be guaranteed.

A review of the place of such a theology of the Cross in the whole development of Christian tradition[41] reveals its potential, not only to inspire deeply affective and spiritual bonds of identity with the crucified one of Christian faith, liturgy and proclamation, but also to become the stimulus and ground for the most profound involvement with the crucified ones of the world. In short, a spirituality of the Cross that holds together the strands of expiation, substitution and exchange, sustains also the praxis of living out with others and for others the crucible of human suffering and the tragedies of both of personal and social existence.

Ministry under the Cross is truly a ministry at the heart of the world. Maintaining this place for itself is a question, not only of right praxis, but of authentic theological interpretation. It is one of Balthasar's gifts to the task of contemporary Christian interpretation, that he speaks so clearly a language of the Cross.

THE PRIESTHOOD: THE WISDOM AND POWER OF THE CROSS

Like Jesus the Redeemer on the Cross, the Church and her ministry is called to assume a Form that is appropriate to a broken world. The call to the priesthood as an objective ministry in the Church is a call to live the Cross both ecclesially and personally. Election to the priesthood, Balthasar states, is equivalent to being made 'a libation for the sacrifice and the service of faith,'[42] and is a participation in the responsibilities of the Good Shepherd who lays down his life for his sheep (Jn 10:15). Having been entrusted with pastoral office, priests, therefore, are required to give their lives away in configuration to the Priesthood and Person of Christ himself.

The absolute demands of this office weigh heavily on the person who is called: pastoral love takes on the Form of the Cross. Acquiring

---

41 Some authors express reservations concerning those aspects of Balthasar's theology of the Cross which give expression to its dimensions of wrath and terror; cf. Gerald O'Collins, *Interpreting Jesus* (London: Chapman Press, 1983). For a comprehensive study of these themes in Balthasar, cf. M. Johri, *Descensus Dei. Theologia della Croce nell'opera di Hans Urs von Balthasar* (Roma, 1981).

42 Hans Urs von Balthasar, *Christlicher Stand*, p. 268.

this Form of life requires a wholehearted surrender, an asceticism that leads Balthasar to view ministerial priesthood as a state of life.[43] For him this comes to its crystallisation in liturgical office of the priest, when he is called to speak not of and for himself, nor by his own strength, but to stand in the place of another to become an *alter Christus*. The words 'This is my Body' and 'I absolve you' disclose the transcendent realities which interweave with the pastoral, routine functions of priesthood and reveal the depths of involvement with God to which priesthood finds itself drawn.[44] The mysteries of the Lord's eucharistic self-giving love unfold in the life of his ministers: like him, they are to be taken and blessed, broken and given, not only in terms of liturgical gesture, but in the praxis of loving the community following the example of Jesus when he washes the disciples' feet on Holy Thursday (Jn 13:1). Such profound self-giving precedes any action or programme, and the seemingly passive life of interior identification with the Lord's passion is in fact the expression of a most highly active willingness for self-sacrifice. Here the Christian priest finds the *apologia* for a life of intercession and vicarious love: here the Christian priest finds the measure of the praxis of the Gospel and is empowered for ministry in a world that often knows only the silence of God and His apparent absence. The martyrdom of indifference which many priests and ministers, and indeed all Christians face in the ordinary fabric of their lives becomes the scenario for a hidden heroism that can only be recognised under the sign of the Son of Man.

Discerning the place and potential for Christian priesthood in the light of a theology of the Cross for Balthasar is a question of seeing ministry under the sign of the Cross. Tracing the contours of priesthood under the Cross is very much part of the art and wisdom of ministry and its praxis.[45]

---

43 Hans Urs von Balthasar, *Kleine Fibel fur verunsicherte Laien* (Einsiedeln: Johannes Verlag, 1980), in which Balthasar reflecting on the nature of office uses the prism of the words of sacred liturgy to highlight the primacy and transcendence of Christ in the office of the Church. For office as state of life in Balthasar's spiritual theology, cf. G.F. O'Hanlon, SJ, 'Von Balthasar and Ecclesial Status of Life', *Miltown Studies* 22: 111–117 (1988).

44 A theme which dominates the writing of Cardinal Basil Hume, Archbishop of Westminster, who in his collection of sermons and addresses on ministerial priesthood recalls priesthood to its transcendent and sacral identity in Christ; cf. *Light in the Lord: Reflections on Priesthood* (Slough: St. Paul Publications, 1991).

45 For Balthasar the kenosis empties out the sacred space for the sacraments and for priesthood in the Church. The place, then, of the priesthood in the Church and in the world is primarily the place of the Cross; cf. Hans Urs von Balthasar, *Neue Klarstellungen* (Einsiedeln: Johannes Verlag, 1979), pp. 120–126.

III

THE MINISTERIAL PRIESTHOOD
AND ITS ECCLESIAL SETTING

INTRODUCTION

Just as the kenosis, or self-giving love of the Son, is at the heart of Christian interpretation of the mystery and reality of God and His engagement with the world, so too, Balthasar understands the kenosis to be the founding vision and essential paradigm of the life and mission of the Church. For Balthasar, Trinity, Christology and Ecclesiology constitute 'a symphonic truth', the 'Form' of the Church's identity taking on an ever-greater approximation to the 'Form' of the Son.[1]
The task of the theologian is therefore to develop interpretative patterns from the whole which then offer appropriate pathways into the exploration of the mystery of both ecclesial and personal engagement with God. These pathways in Balthasar's methodology have their origin and stand in complete continuity with the original 'Form' of revelation and its locus in the experience of the Son.[2]

In Balthasar's Ecclesiology the models and images which provide the starting point and method for elucidating the nature of the Church are those that derive specifically from the 'Form' of the experience of the Son and the contours of his self-giving love.[3]

According to Balthasar, the 'Form' of the self-giving love of the Son in its ecclesial aspect is essentially spousal, and comes to its most explicit expression in the New Testament, when in the letter to the

---

1 Hans Urs von Balthasar, *Die Wahrheit is Symphonische* (Einsiedeln: Johannes Verlag, 1977).
2 Hans Urs von Balthasar, *Einfaltungen. Auf Wegen Christlicher Einigung* (Munich: Kosel, 1969).
3 Hans Urs von Balthasar, *Glaubhaft ist nur Liebe* (= *Christ heute* V/1) (Einsiedeln: Johannes Verlag, 1966); ET *Love Alone: The Way of Revelation*, trans. Alexander Dru (New York: Herder and Herder, 1969).

Ephesians, Christ is said to have loved the Church as his own Body and Bride.[4]

This nuptial consciousness of the Church is in Balthasar's ecclesial understanding, the deepest dimension of her identity. As an essential feature of his Ecclesiology, it shapes in turn the highly typological nature of his ecclesial reflection in which the Marian dimension is central: Mary is the prototype of the Church's responsive faithful love and is the real type and abiding centre of holiness which encompasses the Petrine and ministerial function within the Church. According to Balthasar, the priesthood exists only to nurture, safeguard and make transparent this spousal love of Christ for his Church, and as ministry, remains relative to the feminine Marian centre from which ecclesial faith in Christ flows. It is within this Marian sphere that Office finds its context and meaning; its essential place in the Church represented above all by the Mater Dolorosa and the disciple whom Jesus loved.[5]

In this chapter we shall attempt to elucidate the place of ministerial priesthood in the Church by moving through Balthasar's ecclesiological syntheses in which he interweaves what he calls the 'Christological Constellation' of Mary, Peter and John with what he believes can and must be brought to expression in our categories for both understanding and existentially living out priesthood in the Catholic tradition.

We shall explore in what sense these archetypes of ecclesial reflections remain normative for contemporary ecclesial reflection on priestly ministry, and assess carefully some of the reservations about the symbolic scheme of Balthasar's ecclesial methodology, which is vulnerable to the criticism that it might work as an inhibiting model for the full development of the ecclesial identity of ministerial priesthood.

Finally we shall assess the value of his achievement in recasting ancient and profound themes of ecclesiology in his pursuit of uncovering those Christological principles that remain powerfully

---

4 The antecedents for this in the whole of the Old Testament tradition of the Temple may be seen in as diverse texts as the prophecy of Hosea and the Wisdom of the Song of Songs; also in the New Testament, in the rich symbolism of Cana and the nuptial prefiguration of Calvary. Here I am indebted to the unpublished dissertation of D. Peter Burrows, 'The Feast of Sukkoth in Rabbinic and Related Literature', unpub. diss. (Cincinnati, Ohio: Hebrew Union College–Jewish Institute of Religion, 1974).
5 The Marian dimension of the Church and Office highlighted also by Henri deLubac, *Les églises particulières dans l'Église universelle, suivi de la maternité de l'église* (Paris: Aubier Montaigne, 1971). See also Hans Urs von Balthasar, 'The Marian Principle', *Communio*, XV (1988), pp. 122ff.

constant, if not normative for the Church's self-understanding of her presence and ministry in the world.[6]

THE CONTOURS OF ECCLESIOLOGY

ECCLESIAL RELATIONS

According to Balthasar, ecclesiology is essentially relational. In the first volume of *Herrlichkeit: Schau der Gestalt*, Balthasar discusses the nature of the Church as the medium of God's 'Form' of revelation in Christ. Whilst he affirms that the Church may present herself as an object of enquiry to the historian, to the religious or profane sociologist or to many other specialists, from the viewpoint of her own self-interpretation and awareness:

> The Church has no other form than this relative form, whose function is to point to the supreme form of revelation . . . The Church created from the being of Christ himself has her foundation ultimately in intra-Trinitarian love, poured out on the Cross *pro nobis* and 'for all'.[7]

Therefore such a self-understanding on the part of the Church demands that she see herself more deeply as a medium, as a system of relations whose form becomes comprehensible when it brings together in a coherent manner the elements that as a medium she must communicate and unite.

> That the Church, in order to do this, must unite what appears to be contrary properties should cause no surprise, since her Lord and Head, Christ Himself, brought these properties together, not by happy chance, but according to the structure of his own being; namely, the perfect transparency with which God reveals himself in him and the likewise transparency with which he reveals man as such.[8]

For Balthasar, a Church true to herself lives according to the structure

---

6 For an extensive treatment of these themes of ecclesiology, cf., M. Kehl, *Die Kirche: Eine Katholische Ekklesiologie* (Würzburg: Echter Verlag, 1992).
7 Hans Urs von Balthasar, *Herrlichkeit, vol I*, (Einsiedeln: Johannes Verlag, 1967), p. 557.
8 Ibid., p. 559.

of the being of Christ himself, namely the perfect transparency with which Trinitarian love is revealed in him and which he reveals to us in its turn. Moving on this level of the mystery of the Church as *communio*, Balthasar traces the contours of ecclesial reality out of the lineaments of the reality of the Incarnate, crucified and risen Lord.[9]

For him this 'Form' provides, not merely the boundaries within which ecclesial interpretation takes shape, but also the dynamism of relations through which the Church opens up, from its origin in Trinitarian love, into the world to which it is sent.

The Church, then, in Balthasar's vision is fundamentally born out of the utmost love of God for the world and is itself a relationship of solidarity and love. The language of the Cross in interpreting the most profound depths of ecclesial relations, reveals the lengths to which solidarity in love will go. The kind of community opened up for the Church is none other than the original cell of Christian community, gathered round the Cross, the Church of Mary and John, returning to her origins in Golgotha love. The Church finds the principle of all her relationships in the kenosis of the Son and the *communio* formed within the gift of himself, for the Father's sake and for the life of the world.

For Balthasar, in order to hold this view of ecclesial relations and its origins as love in the event of the Cross, it is essential to sustain the horizon of Trinitarian faith as the primal hermeneutic for ecclesial interpretation. The synthesis of kenosis, love and ecclesial life can only be maintained by staying within the boundaries of crucified love, for Balthasar, the narrow way, and the only way for theology to proceed authentically.

KENOSIS AND COMMUNITY

The relational dimension of the Church's identity is brought to its full disclosure in the language of the Cross. Balthasar describes the whole mystery of the accessibility of Triune love as the very content of the self-giving love of Jesus, and speaks of the opening of the heart of Jesus as a surrendering of what is most intimate and personal for public use; i.e. the open, emptied space of kenotic love is accessible for all.

It is on the Cross that the boundlessness of divine love can achieve so wide a stretching. In the words of Cyril of Jerusalem: 'God has

---

9 *Communio* is a key concept in Balthasar's Ecclesiology, integrating the diversity of ecclesial functions and charisms with the essential mystery of the Church as a communion of love. For a detailed account of the role and limits of models and images in ecclesiology, cf. Avery Dulles, *Models of the Church* (New York: Doubleday, 1974).

opened wide his arms on the Cross in order to span the limits of the earth's orb.'[10]

In *Mysterium Paschale*, reflecting on the relation of the Church to the Passion, Balthasar shows how the Gospel tradition discloses the self-giving of Jesus as not simply an attitude, but an integrally human enactment carried out precisely by virtue of the bodiliness which discloses in a deeper way the identity between the Person of Jesus and his soteriological function. Jesus, Balthasar points out, is at once the disposer (initiating the Eucharist and the New Covenant in his blood) and the disposed of (in obedience to the Father's will that he should be handed over).[11] The Church is born out of the mystery of love between Father and Son that in the Spirit embraces the world: Her essence, all that is Christological and soteriological in her meaning, her community, liturgy and life, are essentially rooted in the mystery of the Triune love for the world, identical now with the self-giving love of the Son, revealed on the Cross and unfolding in the life of his Body, the Church:

> The Body given is the place of the new institution of the covenant of the new gathering of the community: room, altar, sacrifice, meal, community and spirit all at once.[12]

An insightful parallel to this vision of ecclesial relation is developed by John Navone, SJ, for whom the self-giving God revealed in the self-giving Messiah, is shown to be the foundation for 'the dynamism of our charity and hope in the service of the divine and human communion.'[13] The kenosis of the Son is therefore to be understood as the origin of communion, of *koinonia* and *diakonia*.

> The God of Christians is a community (*koinonia*) of the triune communion whose self-giving kenosis serves human kind by transforming us into self-giving and serving persons for the fullness of life in that communion with all others. The triune God's self-giving service is for a universal community (*koinonia*) without limits.[14]

10 Hans Urs von Balthasar, *Mysterium Paschale* (Edinburgh: T. & T. Clark, 1990), p. 130.
11 Ibid., p. 12.
12 Ibid., p. 131.
13 John Navone, SJ, *Self-Giving and Sharing: The Trinity and Human Fulfillment* (Collegeville, Minn.: The Liturgical Press, 1989), p. 41.
14 Ibid., p. 42.

The notion of kenosis as the transforming and integrating principle of true and full *communio*, in the context of Balthasar's ecclesiology, becomes the ground of the Church's understanding of her *diakonia* and its place within the ecclesial relations. For Balthasar, it is within the Form and response of self-giving love that the *diakonia* of office and everything institutional has its genuine place.

Therefore, in Balthasar's view, office as an integral dimension of communion, needs to be seen as essentially in relation. This has a twofold aspect, both necessarily interconnected. One relates to the Trinitarian structure of love in the Church, necessarily that of kenosis and therefore understood as a gift, a grace, as part of Jesus' self-giving love for the Church. The other relates to the mission of that love towards the world, a kenosis again of love that not only hands itself over, but is handed over for the sake of all. The dynamic of the one who both offers and who is offered,[15] is seen clearly again here. Office, having no form of life of its own, is always to be taken in relation to the Form of the sent Son, who not only unconditionally gives himself, but is himself unconditionally given by the Father for the sake of all.

Balthasar develops his whole theology of ministry, institution and office in the light of this fundamental insight of the relational and kenotic nature of ecclesial reality. How Balthasar proceeds both to integrate and uncover these interweaving patterns of ecclesial relations has to do with his perception of this pattern at the very heart of the witness and structures of the New Testament itself. Ultimately, he finds there the access to the living tradition of the Church, an archetypal participation in Christ's all-sustaining experience of God, which he believes provides the Form and pattern of relations that remain a constant of the Church of Christ. This 'handing over', from its very beginnings, is seen to be at once ecclesial and Christological, liturgical and ministerial. It remains a source from which the Church of Christ need never withdraw.[16]

For Balthasar, the Church grows as a body not by moving away from its origin, but by allowing that origin to be present each moment in the power of the Holy Spirit which has been given to it. Balthasar perceives an immediacy in these origins that sustain ecclesial relations with the dynamic that at its beginnings rose out of the unfathomable experiences of Jesus Christ.

---

15 See above, Chapter II.

16 For clarification of the 'time' of the Church and the sense of contemporaneity and immanence of Christ's sustaining presence in her life and mission, cf. Hans Urs von Balthasar, *Herrlichkeit, vol. III/2* (Einsiedeln: Johannes Verlag, 1969), pp. 175–188.

We are and remain members of the Church, branches of its tree, nourished by the sap of its total experience, which ultimately rise up out of the unfathomable experience of Jesus Christ. It is in these powers which work in us that we should trust, for these too mediate to us, the way to him who is himself true immediacy.[17]

This immediacy is not in Balthasar's view an abstract theological perception, but is a concrete unfolding of experiences of Jesus that remain normative for the Church, experiences that have continued to shape ecclesial response and can never be merely a matter of past history for Christian reflection and praxis. Through the Incarnation, the eternal Son of the Father has entered the world of human relations. The historical human relations of the Incarnate Son are in an ecclesial sense, perpetuated within the life of the Church and become intrinsic dimensions of her being and function.[18] It is Balthasar's unique and creative grasp of these relational depths of the Church that is the key to his Ecclesiology and his theology and spirituality of office.

CONSTELLATION AROUND JESUS

A DYNAMIC PROCESS

Integral then to both Balthasar's Christology and Ecclesiology is the concept of 'the Christological constellation', the concrete historical relationship which the Incarnate Son entered into and which remains the paradigm of subsequent relationships in and with Christ. This is particularly true of ecclesial relationships[19]

According to Balthasar, it is impossible to detach Jesus either from his Trinitarian relationships or from the human group that form a totality with him. As the sent Son of the Eternal Father, he does not merely perform before us the drama of eternal love; he makes us participants in the drama. It is in the flesh and blood reality of Jesus that the Trinitarian relational love enters into the world of human relationships. Therefore it is never a matter of 'Christ alone', a

17 Hans Urs von Balthasar, *Klarstellungen* (Freiburg-im-Breisgau: Verlag Herder KG, 1971) ET John Riches, *Elucidations* (London: SPCK, 1975), p. 82.
18 Ibid., pp. 74–78.
19 For Balthasar's most comprehensive treatment of his concept of the Christological constellation, cf. Hans Urs von Balthasar, *Der antiromische Affekt* (Freiburg im Breisgau: Verlag Herder, KG, 1974); ET Andre Emery, *The Office of Peter and the Structure of the Church* (San Francisco: Ignatius Press, 1986), pp. 131–172.

Christology only of abstraction, but of the real Christ in his constellation.

> All men are interrelated in a human constellation. One sole human being would be a contradiction in terms, inconceivable even in the abstract, because to be human is to be with others. The God-man, Jesus Christ, is no exception – as God as well as Man he exists only in his relation to the Father in the unity of the Divine Holy Spirit.[20]

Thus the Trinitarian relational foundation of Jesus' human life and ministry are the ground and the inner-determinant of his relations to others, for he stands as an indivisible whole within a constellation of his fellow men. Balthasar understands this constellation of relationships as essential and not accidental to his being and acting: 'He cannot be detached from his constitutive human group, though this fact in no way infringes upon his sovereign position.'[21]

At the centre of the constellation immediately around Jesus himself, are his Mother and his Apostles, most significantly Peter, John and Paul. 'These figures,' Balthasar affirms, 'belong to the constellation of Jesus and are consequently integral parts of Christology.'[22] They are also intrinsic to ecclesiology, for they are real symbols of the Church, and in that sense, mediatory figures through which the 'Form'[23] of Christ is imprinted upon the whole People of God.

Through the work of the Holy Spirit, the Incarnate Son's historical human relations remain normative and operative within all subsequent ecclesial relationships. For Balthasar the constellation, inseparable from the real historical Jesus, is incorporated together with himself into his Church.

The archetypal experiences of the constellation have become the foundation of the Christian life and mission:[24] A real and vital relationship connects the unfolding experience of faith with the archetypal experience that beneath all empirical and historical development, sustains the essential living tradition of the Church. Furthermore, the archetypal experience of the primary constellation is that which constitutes the consciousness of the Church, which in all its concrete differentiation, i.e. hierarchical structure and diversity of

20 Ibid., p. 137.
21 Ibid., p. 136.
22 Ibid., p. 137.
23 On Balthasar's use of 'Form', see above, Chapter I.
24 Hans Urs von Balthasar, *Herrlichkeit, vol. I*, pp. 301ff., in which Balthasar explores the archetypal experience of ecclesial reality.

charisms, participates in the common treasury of the *Communio Sanctorum*.

It is Christ who makes the Church as a whole participate in this experience, uniting each member of the Church directly to himself and yet, at the same time, mediating between individual members and uniting them to himself through others.

The building up of the life of the Church through the different relationships, charisms and offices, is therefore understood as a dynamic process, already existing within the constellation around Jesus, and carried through to fulfilment in the Form of the Church and its development.

For Balthasar, the Church's life and mission is a continuation of an archetypal experience of Christ that is established within the Church as a permanent and normative feature of her existence. The Church is the more immediate space in which the Form of Christ shines, not as a bare and isolated figure, but in community, a living reality that once lived as a historical reality.[25]

The concrete and historical 'Form' of Christ, in Balthasar's view, can never be outgrown and is a source of relationship and love from which the Church need never withdraw.

MARY, PETER AND JOHN

The structure of the relationships that constitute the archetypal experience of the Christological constellation is represented by the relational constellation of Mary, Peter and John. These figures are considered by Balthasar to be ever present in ecclesial relations as the concrete principle of love that co-exists in the intimate holy bond of *communio* which is the Church. Through this symbolic prism the Church is closely bound to the life and attitude of Mary, whose interiority reveals the hidden, nuptial consciousness of the Church, an all-embracing dynamic of ecclesial life that is served and protected by the Petrine Office. The mediation between the Church of Love and the Church of Office, finding its locus in John who, intimately linked to both Mary and Peter, points out the exact place of Office within ecclesial reality, i.e. standing under the Cross in place of Peter and on his behalf, John receives the Marian and faithful Church.

By interweaving this rich symbolism into his Ecclesiology, Balthasar

---

25 Cf. Hans Urs von Balthasar, *Spiritus Creator* (= *Skizzen zur Theologie III*) (Einsiedeln: Johannes Verlag, 1967), p. 309, in which Balthasar shows how the receptivity of the Church to Christ's informing action is the ground of her ministry and mission.

attempts to present the foundation of the Church's life and unity as an all-embracing reality that integrates not only Marian interiority and holiness, but the Petrine visibility and institutional frailty which cannot be separated from each other.

The primal and mysterious continuity that sustains the essential chain and which holds sway in the life and indeed frailty of the Church, is fundamentally the Marian dimension. The place of Mary within the Christological constellation is not only one of obvious chronological primacy, but one that is theological and axiomatic for the whole of ecclesial identity and response.

In line with the teaching of *Lumen Gentium*,[26] which perceives Mary to be the prototype and image of the Church, Balthasar understands the whole Marian experience as standing in integral relationship to both Christology and Ecclesiology. The continuity between Mary's experience and the Church's continuing experience as Bride and Mother grounds all other dimensions of ecclesial existence in the totality of the mystery of Christ. In this sense, Balthasar continually speaks of the Church as the crystallisation of Triune love in and for the world; Jesus taking flesh in the womb of the Virgin Mother and subsequently in the Motherhood of the Church, continues to be brought forth into the world that is so loved.

For Balthasar, it is precisely this Trinitarian and Christological truth that makes sense of the Church's presence in the world and her fragmentation in history.

> When Mary and Peter enter into relation to this unity in their particular ways, they do so as commissioned by the Lord and for his service. It is only because Christ unceasingly offers himself to and within the Church in the Eucharist, that he is called 'the fullness of him who fills all in all' (Ephes. 1:23).[27]

Naturally, therefore, the Marian motherliness as well as the Petrine pastoral care must be patterned after the Christological model of self-sacrifice.

Balthasar seeks to integrate these different dimensions of ecclesial reality by focusing on the Marian *fiat* in its truly unlimited availability as the fundamental stance of ecclesial faith and response. He

---

26 *Lumen Gentium*, ed. A. Flannery OP (Collegeville: Liturgical Press, 1975), Chapter VIII, 'The Role of the Blessed Virgin Mary, Mother of God, in the Mystery of Christ and the Church'.
27 Hans Urs von Balthasar, *Der antiromische Affekt*, p. 205.

understands Mary's 'Yes' to be fully representative of both the Old and New Covenants and of the obedient readiness of the Church in her ministry and mission.

Mary is the true Daughter of Zion; she gives her consent to the Incarnation, her 'Yes', summing up all the faith aⁿd obedience of Israel from Abraham onwards, integrating the Old Covenant with the New, Judaism with the Church.[28] Her 'Yes' at the Annunciation is an assent, too, on behalf of all creation, all mankind, in which the wedding between heaven and earth, the spousal relationship, prefigured in Old Testament biblical faith, between God and human nature, now takes place, not as an invasion but as love freely offered and freely responded to in the consent of Mary.

The marriage of divinity and humanity becomes then a real two-sided mystery of love through the bridal consent of Mary acting for all the rest of created faith.

And above all, for Balthasar, Mary's 'Yes' to the ministry and finally the Cross of her Son brings into even clearer focus how Christian and ecclesial response participate in the Marian obedient readiness to let God's will and ways be done. This readiness Balthasar understands to be a dynamic that can never be extinguished from Christian consciousness.

At the origins, in the very heart of the Incarnation event, stands Mary, the perfect Virgin who let it be, who consented physically and spiritually to a maternal relationship with the person and also the work of her Son. This relationship might change more and more as Jesus grew and developed his independent personality, but would never be extinguished.[29]

For Balthasar, Marian consent is the fundamental attitude of all Christian faith and mission, its unlimited generosity given over to the whole Church, not only as the model of Christian faith, but as the dynamic form of the life of the whole Church. Balthasar writes:

The Marian fiat in its truly unlimited availability is by grace, the bridal womb, Matrix and Mater, through which the Son of God becomes Man, and that it is by this 'Fiat' that he also forms the universal Church. By the power of the boundless triune God, this 'Fiat' opens up the boundaries of earthly time in advance (in anticipatory redemption in the case of the Immaculate Conception)

28 Ibid., p. 188.
29 Ibid., p. 137.

so that what is earthly and temporal – whether Mary, her Son or the Church – should not place any fundamental obstacle to God's indwelling but should be *infiniti capax*.[30]

The invitation to participate in Mary's believing and loving relation to her Son and her openness to God, is an ecclesial mystery which unfolds from the *pro nobis* of the Trinitarian foundations of Christian love, and is at the heart of Mary's surrender to and never failing readiness (*Bereitschaft*) for the mystery of God's involvement with and for us.

Mary's physio-personal experience of the child who is her God and her Redeemer is unreservedly open to Christianity. Mary's whole experience, as it develops from its earliest beginnings, is an experience for others; for all.[31]

By relativising the hierarchical structure of the Church to the primacy of the Marian, feminine principle, Balthasar remains true to his dictum: 'Before men were placed into office, the whole Church was present in Mary.'[32] The significance of this primal feminine image of the Church for ministerial priesthood lies in its Christological foundation, in recalling the Church to her origin in Christ who gives his life away to her, and to the place of Mary who, together with John, integrates as with a 'protective mantle',[33] the visible and institutional dimensions of the Church with the inwardness of love.

According to Balthasar, the biblical image which most vividly expresses the place of ministerial priesthood within the feminine Marian Church is the Johannine scene of Mary and John at the foot of the Cross. Here, for Balthasar, we are given insight into the mystery of the Church, the relations of the first cell of the Christian community, gathered around and finding its life in the Crucified Son. Here, too, we find the theological synthesis that integrates all other strands of ecclesial self-understanding, e.g. a 'nuptial consciousness' of love between the Lord and his Spousal Church, his Body and his Bride, symbolised in the birth of the Church from the wounded side of Christ.

In *Sponsa Verbi*,[34] in a chapter devoted to exploring the 'personality'

---

30 Ibid., p. 172.

31 Cf. Hans Urs von Balthasar, *Theodramatik, vol. II/2* (Einsiedeln: Johannes Verlag, 1976), pp. 273ff., in which Balthasar develops Mariology in the light of the soteriology of the Incarnation.

32 Hans Urs von Balthasar, *Klarstellungen*, p. 72.

33 Ibid.

34 Hans Urs von Balthasar, *Sponsa Verbi* (= *Skizzen zur Theologie II*) (Einsiedeln: Johannes Verlag, 1960).

of the Church, Balthasar uncovers the rich layers of the biblical and patristic tradition of the image of the birth of the Church from the death pangs of the crucified Lord.[35] This theological truth about the *persona* of the Church is, he suggests, a piece of theological logic that is constantly required to be brought into ecclesial interpretation if it is to remain true to the original Form of the Church, and to keep in their rightful context and place all other forms and structures of Church life.

At the foot of the Cross, Mary personifies the Church as described by Paul: 'holy and without blemish', corresponding fully to the 'masculine' subjectivity of Christ through God's grace and the overshadowing of the Holy Spirit. The Church is imaged as flowing forth from Christ, born from the New Adam, Bride because she is Body. In Balthasar's development of this imagery, Jesus on the Cross, the Head and the Bridegroom, gives himself up for love of his bridal Church, and the Church in Mary is receptive to this gift. The theological truths of the *persona* of the Church are enshrined and concretised in the person of Mary. As 'real symbol' of the Church, she is understood as the Church's embodiment and personification.[36]

Mary at the same time, in allowing the Head of the Church to take flesh in her, is the prototype of the fruitfulness and motherhood of the Church, who in turn delivers Jesus from out of herself into the world. The Marian bridal motherhood identity becomes in Balthasar's typology the paradigm both of who the Church is and of what the Church does.[37]

Mary standing with John and their reciprocal bequeathing corresponds, in Balthasar's intensive symbolic and meditative eyes, to the unity of the immaculate heavenly Church with the still struggling earthly Church. John, standing under the Cross in place of Peter and on his behalf, symbolises the visible Church and is entrusted with the sanctity of the original and ideal Church. He represents Office as that which unites pastoral authority with love.

The Real Presence in and to the Church of Mary, John and Peter remains all-pervading in ecclesial reality, and according to Balthasar, is there to determine the shape and context of ecclesial relations and their development in history.[38]

As Bride, the Church does not stand over and against her Lord, but draws close to him within the nuptial consciousness of her Eucharistic

35 Ibid., pp. 116ff.
36 Ibid., p. 132.
37 Ibid., p. 118.
38 Ibid., p. 137.

life, when she is renewed in love, as she awaits the final coming of the Bridegroom. Mary is given to us as a prototype so that the Church may never forget the depths of her nuptial mystery. Office in the persons of Peter and John is given to love and to foster the Church in this very dimension of her being.[39]

THE PLACE OF OFFICE

THE HUMILIATION OF OFFICE

The Peter-John relationship then, in Balthasar's Ecclesiology, becomes the place to which ministerial priesthood can make its way back to find its origins and its dynamism as both 'Office' and 'Love'. Within the hermeneutical circle of Mary, Peter and John, priestly spirituality can find a way of making sense of its institutional vulnerability by which it comes to grasp its priestly vocation as a call by God to interpret Golgotha love to a broken world, not only in what can be said, but in what can be lived.[40]

Balthasar likewise sees the priesthood as having constantly to find its way back to Mary and John in order to understand the Petrine dimensions of Office. Coming into the light of crucified love, the authority of pastoral Office comes to be perceived as having its ground only in the power of the Cross, the 'absolute night' of crucified love in which authority and Office with Peter emerges, humbled and transformed. Nailed to the Cross, Office and Institution appears in its aspect of love, only by way of finding its place with Mary and John. Only in the place they occupy can the humiliated Peter find his roots and identity again: This Form of Peter illumines forever the place and identity of Office-holders in the Church.[41]

The Peter-John constellation and the sphere of their reciprocal experience can continue to illumine the experience of those called to

39 Balthasar, together with deLubac and Bouyer, finds here the roots of the idea of the 'Fatherhood' of the ministerial priesthood; cf. H. deLubac, *Les églises particulières dans l'Église universelle, suivi de la maternité de l'église*; Louis Bouyer, *Women in the Church* (San Francisco: Ignatius Press, 1982); and Hans Urs von Balthasar, *Der antiromische Affekt*.

40 This was the subject of a paper by the English Dominican theologian John Farrell, given first to the priests of the Archdiocese of Westminster in the light of the demands of urban, and especially inner-city ministry. The paper was subsequently published as 'The Priest at Golgotha', *Priests and People*, 3 (November, 1989), pp. 377–383.

41 For the place of the Petrine Office in the context of the holiness of the Church, cf. Hans Urs von Balthasar, *Der antiromische Affekt*, pp. 172–183.

Office, not only because they represent the creative tensions of the interplay of Office and Love, Institution and Spirit in the life of the Church, but primarily because they provide a way of *living* through the creative tension. By providing access to the contours of the original ecclesial experience, the constellation image continues to sustain those torn by the expectations of Office and the humiliation of defeat, by providing an horizon of loving the Church that embraces the frailty of the human response within the original 'Form' of the all-embracing Marian dimension response of Love, that Office can never attain, but exists only to serve humbly.

Petrine Office, in so far as it demands too much, also reveals the greater love that is taking shape within the frailty of the human response.[42] It is this essential paradox of Office that Balthasar's ecclesial method seeks to elucidate and keep before theological reflection as a reality that cannot be evaded in the interpretation and the praxis of Christian priesthood.

There is no doubt that this vision of priestly ministry implies a definite concept of the Church, in which an Ecclesiology of institution cannot be separated from an Ecclesiology of communion. From the viewpoint of Balthasar, it is essential for Catholic tradition constantly to affirm the necessary relationship between the hidden nuptial consciousness of the Church and her visible communion. The role and function of priesthood as part of the institutional visible dimension of ecclesial reality is precisely as an instrument of unity and love within the sphere of communion, a point taken up by the International Theological Commission on Priestly Ministry, when it declares:

> For the Catholic Church an ecclesiology of communion cannot be separated from an ecclesiology of institution – institution being not understood as merely juridical but as giving structure as vital and spiritual.[43]

INSTITUTION OF GRACE

Balthasar's ecclesial view of priesthood stands in contrast to an Ecclesiology that starts with an empirical and sociological description of priesthood as simply a matter of a natural development within the

42 A recurring theme in Balthasar's elucidation or treatment of the Petrine Office.
43 'The Priestly Ministry', in *The International Theological Commission: Texts and Documents, 1969–1985* (San Francisco: Ignatius Press, 1989).

organisation of the Church of a form of leadership that in time accrued to itself a sacral and cultic image.[44]

Whilst it is clear that the sociological and organisational aspect of the development of ecclesial ministry is an important dimension to understanding its present state and any potential it may have for further development, its intrinsic theological meaning and content cannot be so arbitrarily discerned.

The works of Balthasar and Schillebeeckx exemplify these divergent tendencies within Catholic theology since Vatican II on questions of Ecclesiology and the future shape of the Church and her ministry.[45] Whereas Schillebeeckx seems to be attempting to rebuild theology from foundations in contemporary experience and praxis, Balthasar offers a comprehensive theological system in which doxology and not praxis is the keynote, and in which the full sweep of the Church's thinking takes priority over the particular development.[46]

The theology of Schillebeeckx is one that seeks to foster the prophetic character of the Christian community. It is multi-disciplinary, secularly involved and characterised by an innovative repertoire of approaches and methods within the theological agenda.[47]

This is evident from the direction and forcefulness of Schillebeeckx's writing on ministry where he sees the task of theology to stand in creative and critical relationship to tradition and where the praxis of the faith community is the source and sphere of its continuing theological interpretation and reflection. He describes the consequences of this for the praxis of ministry as:

> . . . a practical and hermeneutical or prophetic task . . . By this I mean that the community along with its ministers places the Christian tradition of practice and experience within the experiential and conceptual horizon (analyzed and interpreted in a critical way), by those who live within a pastoral unit . . . this means that the community and thus its leaders no longer locates the meaning of life and religious needs so exclusively in the liturgy and the Sacraments, which are more than the obvious principles or moments in the formation of communities and no longer an obligation.[48]

44 Cf. Hans Urs von Balthasar, 'Priester des Neuen Bundes', *Pneuma und Institution*, (Einsiedeln: Johannes Verlag, 1974), pp. 340–368.

45 These contrasts are considered in an article on the development of Catholic theology since Vatican II by John McDade, SJ, 'Catholic Theology in the Post-Conciliar Period', in *Modern Catholicism: Vatican II and After*, ed. Adrian Hastings (London: SPCK, 1991).

46 Ibid., p. 429.

47 Ibid., p. 430.

48 Edward Schillebeeckx, *Ministry: Leadership in the Community of Jesus Christ* (London: SCM Press, 1981), p. 137.

It is thus in the light of the present ecclesial experience and praxis that the past is retrieved. On its own, tradition cannot be hermeneutically related to the present situation, but must constantly be considered in the light of the signs of the times.

Clearly, Schillebeeckx is concerned with fidelity to the Gospel and to the values of the Kingdom in his constant theological search for an authentic Christian engagement with the world. The great strength of this position on the development of the Church and her ministry is that it allows for a coherent language of Christian engagement with the world and does so in conformity with the vigour and radicalism of the Gospel. Its weakness, perhaps, lies more in what it fails to speak of and give expression to from the depths of Christian experience, i.e., the power of the archetypal and original experience that continues to give life to the Church and her presence in the world.[49]

The tension between what can be said and what must be said is expressed here: Schillebeeckx responding to the stimulus of the signs of the times pushes theology towards the possibilities of Christian interpretation. Balthasar experiencing the power of the tradition, its symbols and language, recalls Christian reflection to what must be said, to that which remains beyond the planning and programmes of the Christian Church.

In the context of the place and structure of Orders within the Church, it is the received pattern of ecclesial relations that in Balthasar's view, holds precedence over what we say and do about its future shape. Balthasar ultimately believes that the development of ecclesial relations cannot be so open-ended, given what he understands to be the boundaries of an original and derivative Form, the constellation of relationships around Jesus which remain normative for the shape and continuing development of Christian and ecclesial community.

While some may want to question the undeniably Marian quality of his ecclesial understanding of Office and may want to question the feminine-masculine polarity of his symbolism,[50] suggesting a certain kind of passivity that ultimately hinders the full development of the ecclesial identity both of men and of women, Balthasar understands the Marian dimension to be essentially one of dynamism. This too has been clearly demonstrated by Ratzinger in his essay on John Paul's

---

49 Schillebeeckx has developed his initial insights into a new hermeneutic for ministry in the contemporary world in *The Church with a Human Face: A New Expanded Theology of Ministry* (London: SCM Press, 1985).

50 Discussed at length in the collection of essays on Balthasar's theological methodology, *The Analogy of Beauty*, ed. John Riches (Edinburgh: T. & T. Clark, 1986).

encyclical, *Redemptoris Mater*,[51] where he shows that the purpose of an authentic Marian ecclesiology is to help the Christian enter into the dynamic quality of salvation.

> Mary offers a key to interpret our present existence . . . Within this framework, indeed, we also recognise who Mary is, who we are, yet only by considering the dynamism aspect of her role.[52]

It is precisely this dynamic aspect of Mary's role which allows Balthasar the creative freedom to develop his images of the relationship between the Church of Office and the Church of Holiness and Love. In Mary, Balthasar finds the representative of the nuptial Church of the new covenant.[53] Peter, representing Office at a distance from the hidden Form of the Church, is brought back to the place of John, where only he can be given the Office of his pastoral vocation. Thus the unity of Love and Office is sealed in Peter's person, marked by the humiliation of Office in the face of the Marian and Holy Church of Love. The engagement of the whole existence of Office and its involvement with the complete surrender to crucified love is a reality of Christian praxis that is unquestionably stressed through Balthasar's use of ecclesial symbols. Through his use of these images, Balthasar gives expression to an important aspect of the embryonic consciousness in the New Testament in relation to the place and context of ministry in the Church. His insistence on the primacy of relations in ecclesial reality, and that these constitute a received tradition does not rule out the exploration of new patterns and structures for Christian ministry. What it does allow is a way of perceiving a pattern in those relationships that needs to be constantly reflected upon and reaffirmed in the Christian ordering of ministry.

51 Hans Urs von Balthasar, *Mary: God's Yes to Man: John Paul's Encyclical 'Redemptoris Mater'* (San Francisco: Ignatius Press, 1987), pp. 43–154.
52 Ibid., p. 21.
53 Ibid., pp. 170–173.

IV

INTERIORITY AND MISSION

INTRODUCTION

In the light of the spirituality of the constellation model of ecclesial relations, Balthasar understands the office of ministerial priesthood as existing on the level of a relationship of love within the Church; the priesthood has no other function than to make transparent the love of Christ for his Church, his Body and his Bride. This is at the heart of the priest's sacramental and liturgical tasks and the foundation of his pastoral work. These tasks entrusted to him 'of building up the Body of Christ'[1] demand the most profound interiority, in the words of Balthasar, a 'state of life'.[2]

In *Priestly Existence*[3] he points out that in the Catholic consciousness, the service of priestly ministry is not compatible with a 'worldly job' and is not at the disposal of any sort of 'theological genetic engineering' which would seek to shape the function of priesthood in relation to the role of secular caring professions or prophetic critics of society. Priesthood has its own distinctive Form which unfolding from the beginnings of Christian consciousness, continues to be true to its origins.

In this chapter we shall see how Balthasar identifies these origins primarily in the person and ministry of Paul, who as part of the Christological constellation remains an archetype of Christian ministry and mission. Here, too, Balthasar perceives the embryonic under-

---

1 A prominent theme in the *Schema* for the Second General Synod of Bishops, 1971, *The Ministerial Priesthood* (Ottawa, Ont.: Publication Service of the CCC, 1971), in which the consecration of the priest is understood as both a gift to the whole community of faith and a source of interior grace and spiritual transformation of the one ordained.
2 Hans Urs von Balthasar, *Christlicher Stand*, (Einsiedeln: Johannes Verlag, 1977).
3 Hans Urs von Balthasar, 'Priesterliche Existenz', *Sponsa Verbi* (Einsiedeln: Johannes Verlag, 1960). Cf. also a number of short articles by Balthasar on Priestly Spirituality, including 'Uber das priesterliche Amt', *Civitas*, 23 (1968), pp. 794–797; 'Zolibatare Existenz Heute', *Pneuma und Institution*, (Einsiedeln: Johannes Verlag, 1974), pp. 369–383; and 'Personne et Fonction', *Parole de Dieu et Sacerdoce*, 1962, pp. 59–77.

standing of Office that later gives rise to the Catholic doctrine of the
Grace of Orders and the concept of Priestly Character.

In the first major speech at the Synod of 1990, the theme of which
was 'The Formation of Priests in Circumstances of the Present Day',[4]
Cardinal Joseph Ratzinger explored in depth the biblical foundations
of the ministerial priesthood. He writes:

> We have seen that the priesthood of the New Testament, which
> appeared first in the apostles, presupposes a true communion with
> the mission of Jesus Christ. The person who becomes a priest is
> grafted into his mission. For this reason, an intimate personal
> relationship with Christ is fundamental for priestly life and ministry
> . . . the priest should be a person who knows Jesus intimately, has
> met him and has learned to love him . . . He should learn to spend
> his life for Christ and for His flock.[5]

In this text we find an example of the synthesis of those dimensions
of priestly spirituality that are considered by Balthasar to be
foundational to Catholic tradition: discipleship and mission –
interiority and pastoral love, all coming together in a life of complete
surrender to the demands of Office, in which the one called to mission
is sent to give what he cannot give by his own strength. He is sent
to act in the person of another, *in persona Christi*. The dynamics that
allow for this understanding of priesthood, Balthasar finds in the New
Testament itself. Within the Form of discipleship and apostolate, where
the mystery of the divine involvement shines forth as the model of the
Church's own existence and of the *raison d'être* of her ministry and
mission in the world.

THE GRANDEUR AND WEAKNESS OF THE PRIESTHOOD

DISCIPLESHIP AND MISSION

Writing about the New Testament roots of the Catholic understanding
of priesthood, Raymond Brown describes how the two figures of disciple
and apostle come together to form the image of the Christian priest:

4 Joseph Ratzinger, 'The Formation of Priests in the Circumstances of the Present
Day', *Communio*, XVI:4 (1990), pp. 626ff.
5 Ibid., p. 626.

If the New Testament picture of the disciple has greatly influenced the spirituality of the priesthood, especially as regards the conformity of life style to the model of Christ, it is the role of the apostle that has shaped the Christian understanding of the priest's ministry for others.[6]

Within the legitimate pluralism of its function, priesthood, Brown affirms, can find its identity and integration in the Christological depths of the traditions of discipleship and mission, which from the beginning shaped ecclesial consciousness:

> Whatever other claim he may make about what he does, in order to know who he is, a priest must be able to join with Paul in issuing the challenge: 'Be imitators of me as I am of Christ'.[7]

According to Balthasar, priesthood is likewise best understood within the light of the twin poles of discipleship and apostolate. The Christian priest lives always between the mission of his office and the intimacy and demand of personal discipleship. For those who are called and sent, their office is so rooted in the very heart of their following that ministry and life can no longer know of any division. The twofold transcendence of Christian priesthood as a stance both towards the Father and towards the world, as interiority and as praxis, is brought into an ever-deepening integration in a life of mission rooted in radical discipleship.

Within this framework, priesthood is viewed as corresponding to the essential structure of Jesus' own ministry in which Jesus traces his mission back to its source in the Father, revealing his own ministry as both unfolding from the Father's love and as a response to that love. Interiority and mission, love and praxis, are therefore intimately related and provide the paradigm of discipleship and mission which continue to shape ministry in Jesus' name.

It may well seem that an emphasis on the historical character of Jesus' choice and call of the Twelve, and the pattern of their association, is an outmoded form of piety that does not address the complexities of the problems of the presbyterate in the modern world. The unique character, however, of the Christian priesthood and its meaning, if it is to have any specifically Christian meaning at all, lies in its historicity – the historical fact that Jesus desired to share his own ministry, and

6 Raymond Brown, *Priest and Bishop* (London: Geoffrey Chapman, 1970), p. 26.
7 Ibid., p. 45.

the significance for the sacred writers that in so doing he invites and *enables* others to share the mystery of his own vocation, thus rooting the continuation of that ministry within the context of the mystery of his own person and presence accompanying the Church 'until the end of time'.[8] Just as in the Old Testament, Israel understood her whole life to be constituted by the divine initiative and election, and the meaning of her history to be defined ultimately in terms of her engagement with God, so too the whole style and language in which the traditions about discipleship are framed, evoke a total and ongoing engagement with and in the divine involvement, now reaching its final form in Jesus.

There are three important aspects of the call to discipleship that emerge from the Gospel tradition:[9] (1) It springs from the initiative of Jesus; (2) The radical and absolute quality of the call; and (3) The dimension of personal relationship and commitment to Jesus. While certain contemporary writers[10] may call into question the validity of intensifying the call to priesthood by relating it so closely to the Gospel call to discipleship, and the appropriateness today of such a radical shape to the ministry which through history it has come to possess (e.g. celibacy, life-long commitment), it cannot be denied that the Church has understood the elements of vocation, divine initiative and radical response as definitive for priestly life, and that as an interpretation of ministry, the Church has striven to remain faithful to it, representing its dynamic and pattern in the ordering of ecclesial life. As Brown points out, the Church has every right to ask her priesthood to ground and root itself in the life of discipleship as presented in the Gospel tradition. The motive, however, cannot be reduced to 'rights' or be simply laws of exigency, however much these have coloured and conditioned the consciousness of the Church. It is nearer the truth to say that the Church has understood herself to have no other alternative than to interpret her priesthood in terms of discipleship. For the priesthood is ultimately a reality she has received from her Lord and not created for herself, a participation and not

8 Cf. Joseph Ratzinger, 'The Formation of Priests', p. 622. Also Henri Crouzel, 'Le Ministère dans l'Église: temoinage de l'Église ancienne', *Nouvelle Revue Théologique*, 104 (1982), pp. 738–748.
9 For what follows, see David Stanley, SJ, 'Call to Discipleship', *The Way Supplement*, January (1982).
10 Illustrated by Anton Houtepen, 'Gospel, Church, Ministry: A Theological Diagnosis of Present-Day Problems in the Ministry', in *Minister, Pastor, Prophet*, ed. E. Schillebeeckx et al. (SCM Press, 1980)

merely a function. This is a reality made clearer still in Balthasar's phrase about priestly life and service as a miracle of grace.[11]

The priesthood cannot then reflect on itself, but upon Christ as its source and fulfilment, particularly if it is to rediscover its identity and its integration both as a call to intimacy and as a call to mission.[12]

A CALL BEYOND THE CAPACITY TO FULFIL

The restoration of the Christological and relational foundations in theological reflection is a major theme in the writings of Pope John Paul II, and underpins in particular his writings and addresses on the ministerial priesthood, in which he shows himself to stand within the line of authentic Christian spiritual tradition, one that unfolds from the Gospel itself:

> Priesthood is not merely a task which has been assigned – it is a vocation, a call to be heard again and again ... In the midst of Jesus' ministry ... he called his first priests individually and by name to preach the Gospel ... and he made them his own companions, drawing them into that unity of life and action which he shares with the Father, in the very life of the Trinity.[13]

In this address, John Paul, in underlining the relational and transcendent meaning of discipleship in the Gospel tradition, directly relates the ministerial priesthood, with its roots in discipleship, both corporately and personally, to the divine involvement, which has always been the Catholic instinct. He justifies this on two counts. First, that this, in fact, does more justice to the data of revelation and to the Gospel tradition than the less transcendent or sacral models that may be offered today to the Church both from within the Church and from without. Second, to the extent that the presbyterate loses touch with its origins and traditions, it runs the risk of losing itself in some sphere which is not that of Christian ministry.[14]

Attempts at reconstructing the structure of the New Testament

---

11 Hans Urs von Balthasar, *Klarstellungen*, (Freiburg-im-Breisgau: Verlag Herder KG, 1971) ET John Riches, *Elucidations* (London, SPCK, 1975), p. 111.

12 The interdependence of intimacy and mission is a theme that emerges clearly in contemporary spirituality of ministry and has become one of the principle *leitmotifs* of the writing of Henri Nouwen, cf. *The Wounded Healer* (New York: Doubleday, 1972); and *Intimacy* (Notre Dame, Ind.: Fides Publishers, 1969).

13 John Paul II, *A Priest Forever* (Dublin: Veritas, 1981), p. 72.

14 Ibid., pp. 73–75.

communities and of the appointment and function of their office bearers, often go beyond the narrow limits of the historical evidence and are often developed to support a pre-conceived thesis.

The loss of a sacral-transcendent identity of the Catholic priesthood in certain theological circles has been accompanied by a heightened awareness of its identity with the presbyterate/elder figure of the New Testament traditions of ministry. This is often achieved at the expense of overlooking the basic continuity of all post-resurrection ministry and mission with the pre-resurrection mission of the disciples. The ultimate basis of the mission remains the same.[15] The polarisation of these originally mutually connected models of Christian office, the one sent by Jesus and the one given by him to oversee the community, has resulted in an impoverished spirituality of priesthood where task and praxis has been thought to be exclusive of interiority and personal identity.

According to Raymond Brown, the fact that priesthood as we now know it has adopted and adapted to itself some of the most prominent ideals and ministries of the New Testament has led to what he terms the 'grandeur and the weakness of the Priesthood'. Grandeur, because the priesthood has come

> ... to enfold a tremendous idealistic wealth – the spiritual ideals of the disciples of Christ, the spirit of dedicated service in Paul, the tried and true virtues of the presbyterate bishop, the dignity of sacramental ministry, associated with the Bread of Life and the cup of the New Covenant.[16]

Weakness, in so far as all of this can be asked of one man: ... more than was asked of any man who played one of the New Testament roles above.[17]

The resolution Brown offers is a return to the common denominator of all ministries in the New Testament, which he sums up as closeness to Jesus Christ and which he identifies with the spiritual realities of priesthood that an older piety tried to give expression to when it spoke of the priest as another Christ.[18] Here Brown attempts to transcend the unnecessary polarisation by a return to an original and integrating dynamic in Christian tradition.

---

15 Cf. Gisbert Greshake, *The Meaning of Christian Priesthood* (Dublin: Four Courts Press, 1988).
16 Raymond Brown, *Priest and Bishop*, p. 44.
17 Ibid., p. 44.
18 Ibid., p. 42.

For Balthasar, the 'grandeur and weakness' of the priesthood lies precisely in the very dynamic of discipleship, in which what is asked of the priest is beyond the human capacity to fulfil. In Balthasar's grasp of the call to office in the Church, this dynamic is intensified. Those called to office are called essentially to go beyond their own limits.

What makes this life possible is only intimacy with Jesus and the *koinonia* created in his love. Person and Office do not, however, stand in tension. Rather, the distance is transcended by the potential of the grace of calling which does not abhor, but rather embraces the frailty of the one called.

According to Balthasar this going beyond the limits of the priest's own personal strength, this stepping into the void, is the hallmark of Gospel discipleship and the originating form of those called through discipleship to mission.

> The man obedient to his mission fulfils his own being, although he could never find this archetype and ideal of himself by penetrating to the deepest centre of his nature, his super ego or his sub-conscious, or by scrutinising his own disposition, aspirations, talents and potentialities. Simon, the fisherman, before his meeting with Christ, however thoroughly he might have searched within himself, could not possibly have found a trace of Peter. Yet the form 'Peter', the particular mission reserved for him alone, which till then lay hid in the secret of Christ's soul, and at the moment of this encounter was delivered over to him . . . was to be the fulfilment of all that, in Simon, would have sought vainly for a form ultimately void in the eyes of God and for eternity. In the form 'Peter', Simon was made capable of understanding the Word of Christ, because the form itself issued from the Word and was conjoined with it.[19]

A life of discipleship roots mission in authentic Christian reality; it guarantees radical ministry and shapes a life of ministry according to the Gospel, a point taken up by Moltmann in his description of the dynamics of discipleship in Christian ministry:

> It is not a matter of our becoming masters through believing that practice makes perfect; what happens is that in and through our openness and suffering God becomes our master. Often he leads us

19 Hans Urs von Balthasar, *Das Betrachtende Gebet* (Einsiedeln: Johannes Verlag, 1957); ET *Prayer*, trans. A.V. Littledale (New York: Sheed and Ward, 1967), p. 49.

where we do not want to go, and breaks the form of our lives . . . so that His Form may come to expression.[20]

When Balthasar writes, in *The Priest I Want*, that there is no other way for the priest to remain faithful to his task than 'by giving up one's whole existence totally to it',[21] he is not speaking of a juridical obligation nor of some extrinsic demand, but out of the depths of the Gospel tradition itself. Like Moltmann, Balthasar understands the language of negation involved in discipleship as serving to highlight the creative, transforming dimensions of a life rooted in following Jesus.[22]

PAULINE CONSCIOUSNESS

ECCLESIAL CONSCIOUSNESS

The paradigm of the Twelve going out in all directions and yet being drawn into the circle of Triune love through their intimacy with Jesus, continues to shape the Catholic consciousness of ministerial priesthood, in which the pastoral vocation is at once ecclesial and highly personal.

The mission of the Christian priest can never then be distanced from the initial configuration to the Person and work of Christ. The communal dimension of the call to ministry likewise cannot be separated from the character of the calling as personal appeal. Balthasar perceives the potential for this synthesis of interiority and mission in the witness of the New Testament itself, particularly in the life and ministry of Paul, who as the other prominent figure in the Christological constellation, provides an archetypal experience for Christian reflection and praxis, particularly in the context of the pastoral vocation.

20 Jürgen Moltmann, *The Passion for Life – A Messianic Lifestyle* (Philadelphia: Fortress Press, 1978), p. 43.
21 Hans Urs von Balthasar, *Klarstellungen*, p. 105.
22 In this perception Balthasar stands within the great strands of Christian tradition, which from its origins understood the way of transformation as a *via negativa*. Cf. also Louis Bouyer, *The History of Spirituality, Vol. I: The Spirituality of the New Testament and the Fathers* (New York: Seabury Press, 1965). Cf. also, Rowan Williams, *The Wound of Knowledge: Christian Spirituality from the New Testament to St. John of the Cross* (London: Darton, Longman and Todd, 1990).

According to Balthasar, Paul represents . . . the passion of Christ to the communities, in the pouring out of his life as pastoral love; he himself becomes a *typos* as he models himself on the type of Christ.[23]

He is the clarification of what will be called Office in the Church.

Authority in the Church, the precise autonomy of which Paul has made plain, theologically as well as pastorally, for all ages of the Church on the basis of his own experience is just as distinctively marked by the Christ Event as was the earlier Peter-John structure.[24]

Balthasar uncovers from the Pauline witness the presence of what he calls an ecclesiastical consciousness in which the personal identity, the very self of Paul the Office-holder, is appropriated into the most profound depths of ecclesial consciousness.[25] The 'I' of St Paul emerges from the deepest consciousness of ecclesial communion in and with Christ.[26] In Galatians 4, Paul actually talks of the community as that which he brings forth in travail, out of himself, identifying his whole life with the good of the Church and the glory of God. His love of the Church is patterned on and arises from the identity in Christ that he lives out in his own anxiety and cares for the communities entrusted to him.

Balthasar emphasises that this 'I' is to be understood in terms of ministry and not psychology. It is in the personal character of Christian ministry, through the 'I' of the minister of Christ, that the mystery of Christ's presence to and in his people, rather than being diminished, is more clearly set forth.[27] Paul's own beautiful description of this dynamic as 'treasure in earthenware jars' expresses most clearly the transcendent dimension of Christian ministry.

Balthasar identifies this process as one in which a new fulfilment of self takes shape, through loss of ownership of self, and a sense of belonging wholly to Christ and the Communion of Saints.

23 Hans Urs von Balthasar, *Der antiromische Affekt* (Freiburg-im-Beisgau: Verlag Herder KG, 1974), p. 159.
24 Ibid., p. 144.
25 Hans Urs von Balthasar, *Herrlichkeit, vol. I* (Ensiedeln: Johannes Verlag, 1971), pp. 354ff., where Balthasar elucidates the Pauline tradition in New Testament ecclesiology.
26 This personal ecclesial consciousness of Paul is explored at length by Balthasar in *Sponsa Verbi*, pp. 137–144.
27 Ibid., p. 138.

For Balthasar this dynamic in both its ecclesial and personal dimensions, comes out most clearly in Paul's use of the personal pronoun.[28] The personal pronoun in Paul is the 'I' of *Christ's* mission; the 'I' transformed into the steward of Christ. It is ecclesiastical; it knows itself as utterly divested of ownership in itself. What is 'best' for Paul is what serves the Church best; and for her sake he continues to live (Phil. 1:23–25).

This 'I'-consciousness is explicable therefore only in terms of mission, its autonomy and authenticity extending beyond the limits of a private consciousness within which Paul continually receives his mission and identity from the Lord who chooses and sends him. This new and radical consciousness, Balthasar points out, consists not in a diminution, still less an extinction, of personal consciousness, but in its being taken along in faith into the consciousness of Christ.

Paul often describes this new appropriation as a transition from consciousness of his own action to a consciousness of God's action taking place within him.

As Balthasar points out, there is an implicit Trinitarian foundation in this view of Christian ministry, the Trinitarian structure of the ministerial 'I' of Christ himself.

> It is because the 'I' of Christ harbours the Father and the Spirit in love, that he can release out of himself the Mystical Body with all its personal members, their mission of sanctification and love. And because the Trinitarian 'I' of Christ wills to dwell in those who love him (John 14:23), the 'I' of Paul is not only dominated by this divine life, but harbours the communities entrusted to him.[29]

Far beyond the potentiality of the personal 'I', the ecclesial 'I' of the office holder has its origins and direction in the deepest level of ecclesial consciousness. Like Paul, the one called to Office is not understood as standing there in the absence of Christ; rather Christ is present to his people in the very place that Office occupies, the place for which Office remains empty.

The ecclesial consciousness which led Paul to experience as costly discipleship the burdens of Office, and as a share in Christ's sufferings, the labours of pastoral love, in Balthasar's view continues to unfold in the dynamics of Office in the Church. He is among many spiritual writers from varying Christian traditions, who perceive in the Pauline

28 Ibid., p. 139.
29 Ibid., p. 140.

witness, characteristics of Christian ministry which remain normative and inspiring.[30]

The task of uncovering the existential dimensions to this archetypal experience of Office is through the very images and concepts that Paul himself uses to interpret and communicate his experience as Pastor.

TREASURE IN EARTHEN VESSELS

The very beautiful description of ministry used by St Paul himself – 'We have this treasure in earthen vessels' (2 Cor. 4:7) – brings the fragile 'I' of the Christian priest into the context of the grace which alone can make sense of the institutional frailty of the Church and her mission. It is a grace which does not ultimately leave untouched the person of the minister, but through his very experience of unworthiness leads him to a more complete surrender to the objective holiness of his office.[31]

Through personal experience Paul comes to realise the simple truth that God's minister must prepare himself by emptying his heart of all personal achievements so that he might become more and more a versatile instrument in the hands of God. It is in the fullness of encounters with Christ that by grace and mercy the Pastor can discover the potential openness of his being towards God, an openness that creates fruitful apostolic involvement with others. The Paul who contemplates and lives for the Lord, who shares in the Passion of Jesus, who is the servant and steward of his mysteries, is the Pastor who loves so deeply his people who can be for him a source both of sadness and tears or of intense joy:

> I have written to you out of much affliction and anguish of heart, and with many tears, not to cause you pain, but to let you know the abundant love that I have for you . . . I have great confidence in you; I have great pride in you; I am filled with comfort; with all our afflictions, I am overjoyed (2 Cor. 2:4).

The paradox of Office that unfolds in the life and ministry of Paul has to do with an experience of weakness which is transformed through

---

30 Cf. Martin Hengel, *The Pre-Christian Paul* (London: SCM Press, 1991); and *Between Jesus and Paul* (London: SCM Press, 1983).

31 Carlo Martini speaks of this process, apparent in Paul's own experience of office, as one of transformation; '. . . the product of a long journey of trials, sufferings, incessant prayer and trust constantly renewed.' *The Testimony of St Paul* (Slough: St Paul Publications, 1983).

the supporting power of Christ himself. This power becomes evident in the continuity of life and ministry; it is a fidelity which weakness would only seem to undermine. The Christian priest is called to discover what his vocation means in such weakness; in this way the 'earthenware vessel' dimension becomes the pretext and indeed the primal motivation for the priest to evoke more deeply in his life the presence of the Lord.[32]

Whilst Balthasar refrains from any attempt at an existential presentation of this important dimension of Christian priesthood, his whole theology of Office is grounded in the idea that for the priesthood to be authentic, the character of crucified love can never be lost sight of, particularly in the fragility of the one called.[33] It is the objective character of Office that challenges the priest as person to enter into loving response to the initiating and saving love of God. Priests as persons are participants in the action of divine love in the world, in so far as they have been received into its movement and have allowed themselves to be given back to the world as signs of Triune love.[34]

It was the disciples who first received most intensely the self-donation of Jesus and who through their inability and failure to respond adequately to and return such love, and by their election for mission within this paradox of Office, became the foil for and the sign of the kenosis, the lengths and endeavours of the love of the Son. Their response was never the measure of the love they received from Jesus, whose 'greater love' is measured on the Cross, revealing that 'the transcendent power is seen to belong to God and not to us' (2 Cor. 4:7).[35]

32 For an application of the Pauline spirituality of ministry to the contemporary needs of priesthood today, cf. Michael J. Buckley, SJ, 'Because Beset with Weakness', in *To Be a Priest*, ed. R. Termilliger (New York: Seabury, 1975), pp. 125–130; also Paul T. Keyes, *Pastoral Presence and the Diocesan Priest* (Whitinsville, Mass.: Affirmation House, 1978), pp. 17ff.

33 Whilst Balthasar does not explicitly enter into existential descriptions of the fragility of those who are called to the burden of office, the whole tenor of his writing reveals his profound grasp of the costliness of discipleship, as well as his vision of the compassion of Christ towards the fragility of his ministers; cf. Balthasar's reflections on Peter.

34 For a spiritual and theological reflection on the priest as person, cf. Robert Lauder, *The Priest as Person* (Whitinsville: Affirmation House, 1981).

35 In Balthasar's theology of election, the Divine involvement always has priority over the human response. Divine initiative and the dynamics of the greater love of God is at the heart of the paradox of following and of Office in the Church.

PERSONAL AND ECCLESIAL IDENTITY

Thomas O'Meara, in his study of theology of priesthood, has pointed out that the type of spirituality described above is so markedly personal that it fails to reflect the essential dynamism of ecclesial ministry and speaks of it as a romantic and ideal version of Christian praxis.[36] Citing the example of the Curé d'Ars and others belonging to this personal School of Spirituality, he describes the profoundly personal and ascetic image of holiness as a less than adequate model of Christian priesthood, which needs to be seen in the light of its new challenges towards integration with other ministries and its rightful place in the secular world.

The ideas reflected in both O'Meara's presuppositions and conclusions are those that Balthasar identifies with a tendency in contemporary ecclesiology to abandon the dimensions of contemplation and surrender which constitute, in his view, the 'soul' of Catholicism.[37]

The light that shines from the lives of the Saints, however at one level they may seem idealised, throws into sharp relief the 'Christ-Form', the character of which is sustained by the holiness of lives lived out of the Marian 'Fiat' that is at the centre and source of the Church's community and bond.[38] The hierarchical principle, however, is at one step removed – is with Peter, exposed in its humiliation and existing only as service of and subordinate to the Marian principle.

The insight that Office exists only in context of the ecclesial whole must also include that it exists in relation, and as such has both a communal and a personal dimension.

It is the 'personal' that Balthasar believes to be neglected in the more collective consciousness of contemporary ministry. For Balthasar, 'personal' is not to be taken in the sense of a narrowly egotistical, individualistic concept, but is always to be understood in relation. Indeed, it is always ecclesially to be understood in the light of Trinitarian relations, where the intra-Trinitarian relationships of love become the foundations of the divine involvement in the world.[39] Interiority then is intimately related to the 'other'. It is the only basis for authentic and loving praxis. The interiorisation of the character of priestly office then becomes the basis for an evermore fruitful ecclesial identity and mission. The priesthood finds its own truth, that it is not

---

36 Thomas O'Meara, *Theology of Ministry* (Ramsey, N.J.: Paulist Press, 1983).

37 Cf. Hans Urs von Balthasar, *Klarstellungen*, p. 90.

38 See above, Chapter III.

39 Cf. Hans Urs von Balthasar, *Theodramatik, vol. II* (Einsiedeln: Johannes Verlag. 1978), pp. 335ff.

an end in itself, but crystallises, rather, the love of Christ for his Church, the Body and Bride to whom and for whose sake he gives himself away. A strong ecclesial identity includes both a sense of living wholly only for service and a willingness to lose one's own identity to the absolute demands of ecclesial love. This is made possible only by a profoundly personal surrender to the radical call of Christ and of his Gospel.

Therefore according to Balthasar, there *is* a simultaneity of interiority and mission, of ecclesial holiness and personal frailty, power and weakness, the triumph of love and the struggle with sin in the New Testament witness itself.

Balthasar, therefore, sees in the person and pastoral vocation of Paul what might aptly be described as an implicit spirituality of office. Everything presupposed by the Gospel ideas of discipleship is experienced by Paul in his own discoveries of his identity in Christ through the pastoral love of those entrusted to him by the Lord. In his life and teachings as Pastor, Balthasar finds in Paul, one in whom person and office, grace and weakness, service of God and service of others, become uniquely integrated. He is one who grows around God and not his own centre, one who has tried to make the love of Christ the basis of everything. In this Paul becomes a witness *par excellence* to the dynamism of personal spirituality. A radically personal spirituality of priesthood need not be over and against the collaborative model of ecclesial relations. Rather it can be seen as integral to the credibility of Christian ministry in the world which can never be less than fully personal if it is to be truly ecclesial and for others.

GRACE AND ORDERS – A PRIESTLY HEART

PRIESTLY CHARACTER

Clearly what Balthasar is continuing to offer the theology of priesthood is a language of the objectivity of Office, one that rests on the Catholic concept of priestly character. Though it remains an abstract language, the reality it seeks to express is seen here to be wholly biblical and corresponds to the earlier traditions of ministry and service in the community. That it remains problematic for contemporary theology cannot be ignored if the whole question of identity and interiority rests on the way in which theology proceeds as it resolves the question of the character of priestly existence.

Balthasar describes this reciprocity between office and personal identity in the priestly state as a process of so entering into this form 'of the love of the Redeemer who sacrificed himself for all', that it becomes the form of human life.

> One who vows himself to this way of life puts it on like a garment and must strive to adapt himself to its dimensions and requirements.[40]

It is, according to Balthasar, in the existential knowledge of their own insufficiencies, that those called to office from the very beginning, were given the gift of humility which is the foundation of the hierarchical order within the Church and of the character of priestly office. The lesson of Office is to learn to perceive the difference between person and Office, to distinguish between the significance of Office of which the Lord is the only true measure, and the insignificance of the person; in this way the person becomes a worthy minister in the Lord's service.

Balthasar is not alone in discovering the truth and creativity behind the tradition of the notion of priestly character. Kasper reminds us of the essential dynamism of character as one that safeguards the data of Christian faith, in the fact

> . . . that Jesus Christ as head and high Priest of his Church, is himself the primary proclaimer, distributor of the sacraments, and shepherd, who works through the priest . . .[41]

This ontological understanding of priesthood, he adds,

> . . . is a help and a consolation, because priests can say to themselves, that the salvation of their communities and of the people committed to them, does not ultimately depend on their own accomplishments and their own success.[42]

Galot justifies its validity on the grounds that as a dynamic it is ordered only to the mission of the priesthood, safeguarding the Christological foundations of ecclesial ministry, where the priest, for the sake of the Church, becomes indeed an *alter Christus*.

40 Hans Urs von Balthasar, *Christlicher Stand*, p. 255.
41 Walter Kasper, 'Ministry in the Church: Taking Issue with Edward Schillebeeckx', *Communio*, X (Summer, 1983), pp. 185–195.
42 Ibid., p. 189.

The mission of the priest is not carried out from without as if someone is sent by another to express a wish or convey an order. God engraves the mission in the very person. He makes it inseparable from personal being.[43]

Therefore, the ontological nature of priestly character, which is judged by Schoonenberg, Schillebeeckx and others as an unnecessary mystification of what is a functional leadership within the community, is intimately linked to its dynamism in the concrete activities of ministry and mission. As Galot explains:

In the priestly character, consecration and conformity are not for their own sake. They insert themselves into the human being as a project for life and activity.[44]

Character is, therefore, about empowerment for ministry, and far from restraining priesthood into a narrowly ritual existence, Galot maintains, its function in authentic Catholic tradition has been to animate and mobilise all personal resources and powers for the sake of pastoral existence.[45]

The idea that the ontological nature of priestly character is intimately linked to its dynamism as mission is also developed by the Anglican theologian, John Macquarrie, who argues that if Christ himself is the true minister of every Sacrament and the unworthiness of the human agent cannot void Christ's bestowal of grace, then a language must be maintained that gives expression to ministry as a grace or gift bestowed by Christ himself.[46] This abiding truth in the idea of priestly character cannot be easily dismissed as no longer having a place in a renewed theology of ordained ministry. If a new, more personalised language were to emerge, it would need to correspond to the reality that lies behind the traditional language and not deteriorate into a merely functional description of priestly ministry.[47] Macquarrie focuses on two dimensions of priesthood that hinge on the continuation of the notion of character: (1) the distinction without separation of the ordained ministry within the indivisible Body of the Church; and (2) the

---

43 Jean Galot, *Theology of the Priesthood* (San Francisco: St Ignatius Press, 1988), p. 201.

44 Ibid., p. 201.

45 Ibid., p. 208.

46 John Macquarrie, *Theology, Church and Ministry* (London: SCM Press, 1986), pp. 167ff.

47 Ibid., p. 170.

character of priesthood as a vocation that seizes upon the whole of a person's life for its full flowering.[48]

In contrast then to those who view the language of character as elitist and outmoded to the needs of the praxis of ministry,[49] this more dynamic understanding of the character of priesthood has to do with only the mission and not the status of the Christian priest, indeed clarifying what exactly it means for a priest to be a man for others.

It is certainly not to be confused with a certain 'clericalism' which establishes a style of life and separation of priesthood from the life of lay Christians and which does not see ordained ministry in the light of the community and of the Church, but vice versa. It corresponds, rather, to the insight of Karl Rahner when he wrote of the essential responsibilities of the priestly office and its unrelenting demands for personal holiness:

> You are only what you should be as a priest, if you bring your whole life into your vocation ... Your life-work is to establish an ever closer intimacy between yourself and your office ... what you do as an accredited officer in the visible society of the outward Church must be the law of your own personal life. If you try to make the gap between your office and your life one of principle, deliberately maintaining it, if you try to keep yourself to yourself, giving the Church only your fulfilment of particular official duties, then you have violated a basic law of your life and of Christianity, that office and person must be one.[50]

It is significant how the insights into priestly existence implicit in the notion of character have come to the surface in John Paul II's theme of a 'priestly heart' in his teaching on priesthood. In one of his Holy Thursday letters to priests, John Paul writes of the priesthood as a gift of Christ for the community and calls for a rediscovery of priesthood as essentially a service,

> ... through which Christ himself unceasingly serves the Father in the work of our salvation. Such a rediscovery will mean a priestly

48 Ibid., p. 177.
49 Joseph Martos, *Doors to the Sacred* (London, SCM Press, 1981), p. 511; and Richard McBrien, *Ministry* (San Francisco: Harper and Row, 1987).
50 Karl Rahner, 'The Unity of Person and Office,' in *Servants of the Lord* (London: Burns and Oates, 1968).

existence deeply imbued with this sense of identity, a recovery of priestly dignity and the 'availability' proportionate to it.[51]

In using this language for the pastoral ministry, John Paul is affirming the need for the notion of a priestly heart or priestly spirit, to which the traditional doctrine of a priestly character has sought to give expression.

For a contemporary spirituality of the ministerial priesthood, a recovery of what is originally meant by the notion of character might lead precisely to the language of gift and grace found in John Paul's letter and to the vision and experience of priestly existence which makes such a language possible. The pivotal source for such a language and vision of ministry, which Balthasar has perceived in the person and teaching of Paul, is crystallised in that saying which so appropriately expressed the truth about ministerial existence, and what today we might call a priestly heart: 'My grace is sufficient for you; my power is made perfect in weakness' (2 Cor. 12:9–10).

GRACE OF ORDERS

The Grace of Orders is given to the Church to cultivate holiness and as sign that nothing, not even sin, can overcome God's grace. It was the struggle against Donatism that helped the Western Church formulate the doctrine of *Opus Operatum*, the objective existence and influence of grace within a priest despite his unworthiness. But it was explicitly taught in the past by, for example, St. John Chrysostom in his work on the priesthood, in which he says, '. . . everything springs from grace.'[52] Once the priesthood's objective, grace-given character is denied or removed, the way is open for leadership and ministry in the Church, to be interpreted no longer as a miracle of grace, but as defined by human worth and achievement. This view of ministry emphasises the communal recognition of the gifts a man already possesses, ordination as not so much a giving of the Spirit to *make* a man a bishop or presbyter, but an act signifying that this man is acknowledged by the community to be the sort of man who should be its spiritual leader and minister of worship.

Ironically, this view seems to institutionalise the crudest version of justification by works and merits. The Catholic Sacrament of Orders

51 John Paul II, 'Letter of the Supreme Pontiff, John Paul II, on the Occasion of Holy Thursday, 1979' (London: Catholic Truth Society, 1979).
52 St John Chrysostom, In 2 Tim 2:4; PG 62:612.

with its insistence on the Spirit's gift through the hands of the Apostles' successor leaves no room for any sense of human merit or achievement.

Vladimir Solovyev, the nineteenth-century Russian writer,[53] speaks of the Sacrament of Orders as an economy in which all is grace and in which, and because of which, the Spirit restrains and overcomes fallen man's need to dominate and create leadership. Balthasar, radically reliant on biblical tradition, gives expression to a vision of the 'economy of grace' in which authority in the Church is expressed in assuming the condition of a slave; existentially it is experienced in the grace and humiliation of office, of the void where there is no one or nothing upon whom to rely, save Jesus himself. The priest can be true to his office only if he humbly acknowledges his dependence on God for all things and cultivates an authentic and penitent acknowledgement of sin and weakness.[54]

Within this context of grace, to be a person 'sent' means to have died with Christ, to have been crucified to the world, and as a dying with Christ, the pattern of ministry and service represents and expresses Christ's own crucifixion in weakness, but his living in the power of God. In becoming a new creation, there is involved not merely a passive transference into Christ, but an active sharing and reception into us of Christ's mission.

All this is from God, Who through Christ reconciled us to Himself and gave us the ministry of reconciliation: that is, God was in Christ reconciling the world to Himself, not counting their trespasses against them, and entrusting to us the message of reconciliation. So we are ambassadors for Christ, God making His appeal through us. (2 Cor. 5:18–20)

Seeing and understanding in discipleship what has been done for him and coming to experience himself as not his own, the priest consequently owes it to his office that he experiences and manifests in his person the essential mark of Christian holiness, a dying to Christ that does not cancel out the disparity between human weakness and divine image and form, but gives the disparity a new meaning and power as 'God making his appeal'. Raymond Brown, examining this dimension of the Pauline understanding of apostolic service, writes:

53 Vladimir Solovyev, 'God, Man and the Church', in *The Spiritual Foundation of Life* (London: SPCK [Fellowship of St Alban and St Sergius], 1974).
54 I am indebted for these insights to John Saward in a talk given at Cambridge University Chapel in 1989.

He is an apostle because he has been sent by the risen Jesus; and in the Jewish notion of apostolate the one sent (*shaluach*; *sheliach*) represents the one who sends, carrying not only the sender's authority, but even his presence to others. Thus Paul as an apostle presents Jesus to men, not only by his preaching: 'We preach not ourselves, but Jesus Christ as Lord, with ourselves as your servants for Jesus' sake' (2 Cor. 4:5); but also by his life: 'It is no longer I who live, but Christ who lives in me: and the life I now live by faith in the Son of God who loved me and gave himself for me.' (Gal. 2:20)[55]

To be an apostle and a servant of the Gospel, the priest must first understand himself to have been given to the Church, chosen out of divine love for the Church, and as such, no longer himself the measure and criterion of the meaning of his ministry, but one who like Paul continually receives mission and meaning from the Lord who chooses and sends him.

What Balthasar offers in his theology of Orders is the perception of an embryonic spirituality of ministry in the earliest traditions of the New Testament itself. This spirituality he identifies as radically Christ-centred and rooted in a Christian consciousness where the 'I' of the Christian minister in all of its frailty reveals the power of Christ and the faithfulness of his promises to be with the Church until the end of time. Far from being the product of a developing sacralisation of ministry in the Church, Balthasar shows that this process operated from the very beginning and that however distorted or narrow the moulding of ordained ministry in its various stages might have become, the synthesis of person and office, call and response, interiority and mission was never lost sight of.

For Christian priesthood to be true to its roots and identity, it cannot move out of this synthesis either into a completely functional or a completely ritualistic concept of its life or meaning. Rather it needs to live out of the tension of its essential 'grandeur and weakness'. In the words of John Saward:

> It is Christ, the eternal High Priest who is present and who acts in Peter and the apostles and in their successors, but in the apostolic minister's very conformity to Christ, in his indelible priestly character, he is humbled, shown up, exposed, he is a pygmy in giant's armour, a fool for Christ's sake, a spectacle to angels and

55 Raymond Brown, *Priest and Bishop*, p. 28.

men. Peter and the apostles, and their successors, embody in themselves the ever greater demands of Christ and the weaknesses of his human representatives. Their mission is just this: to give God the greater glory; to reveal the power of Christ in their very weakness.[56]

Living out of this experience is for Christian priesthood to live out of the paradox of grace. Tracing the paradox of grace with all its themes of particularity and chosenness, of passion and of the triumph of love, is primarily, in Balthasar's view, the task of uncovering the depths of sacred tradition. A priesthood in search of wholeness and holiness, in Balthasar's view, comes to receive this as a gift from tradition itself. Uncovering the contours of sacred tradition is perhaps the first step in attaining the wholeness and holiness of the ministerial priesthood.

56 John Saward, 'Mary and Peter', in *The Analogy of Beauty*, ed. John Riches (Edinburgh: T. & T. Clark, 1986), p. 126.

V

PRIESTHOOD AS A STATE OF LIFE: THE EVANGELICAL COUNSELS AND THE RADICALISM OF THE GOSPEL

INTRODUCTION

The spirituality of the ministerial priesthood, we have come to see, is wholly ordered to its pastoral mission and is, nonetheless, for this very reason a profoundly interior and contemplative existence. Mission and interiority, function and identity, action and contemplation form one complete ecclesial and personal style of life.

Balthasar refers to this theological and spiritual fact of priestly existence as a call to a state of life, that is a life that corresponds entirely to the spirit of the Evangelical Counsels, rooted in a life of radical discipleship and the most explicit form of consecration to the Person of Christ. For Balthasar, if the Church's instinct is to remain that the priest is configured to Christ in his pastoral and spousal identity, then the existential life form of the priesthood needs to correspond to the Form of Christ the Shepherd and Spouse of the Church. Such a Christological identity transcends a merely sociological and functional interpretation of ecclesial ministry and goes beyond even the most legitimate claims on the priesthood for accountability and professionalism that characterise so much contemporary spirituality of the priesthood. Balthasar's starting point, whilst it does not contradict these current concerns for accountability, comes to the whole question of authenticity and pastoral fruitfulness from another angle, which is one of personal consecration and fidelity to an ontological call rather than a set of functions.

This fundamental Christological form is present in every state of ecclesial life and has its roots, according to Balthasar, in the mystery of an ecclesial economy that is inseparable from its Trinitarian origins.

> . . . everything rests on the one and triune love of the Father: in it, the source of all love, there remains the One who makes himself

available. And in the free obedience of the Son, to whom the disciple adheres, the Father's love is manifest to the disciple. Such availability is always sincere love for the world, genuine mission toward the brethren, clear representation of the world before God. Whether this availability is translated into prayer and contemplation, into official, active Church ministry in service to the world, or into a life uniting the two – that is secondary.[1]

Balthasar appeals to this deeper dimension of ecclesial and Christological identity common to all the states of life to establish a fully relational and communal context for understanding what distinguishes and nuances the states in their particularity. The distinctiveness of the priestly state of life lies only in its relationship and meaning to the whole Body of Christ, and it is precisely its uniquely pastoral relationship that demands the response and investment of the whole of the priest's personal identity and existence.

As we come to scrutinise more carefully the lines of Balthasar's thinking, what principally springs from his reflection on the priesthood is his emphasis on both the personal and the transcendent dimensions of pastoral ministry. There is clearly a problematic consideration for a spirituality of priesthood that needs to possess a pastoral vigour and imminence in its self-understanding. In this chapter we shall assess the extent to which Balthasar's transcendent and personal concerns might hold back the fully immanent and pastoral Ascesis that the Church holds out to the ministerial priesthood as the proper sphere of its own identity and mission in the community of faith. In *Pastores Dabo Vobis*, the consecration of the priest is understood in the light of his pastoral mission, and the appropriateness of the spirit of the Counsels is linked towards that pastoral charity which is the essence of priestly life and work. Balthasar certainly moves within this vision and the parallels that emerge between his own seminal thinking on the intrinsic relationship between the priesthood and the Counsels and the insights of *Pastores Dabo Vobis* are striking. Whatever questions might be asked concerning the adequacy of Balthasar's highly idealised and intensely personal approach to the spiritual life and identity of priesthood, it needs to be affirmed that at the heart of his method is the principle that whatever is personal in the community of faith is always to be understood as ecclesial, and that the ecclesial is personal. This notion of 'person in relation' is the cornerstone of Balthasar's

1 *The Von Balthasar Reader* (Edinburgh: T. & T. Clark, 1982), p. 349

ecclesial spirituality and saves him from any serious charge of individualism.

For Balthasar the ministerial priesthood expresses Christ's love for the Church, his Body and his Bride, and is essentially a service of the baptised. From the perspective he offers, ministerial priesthood is a particular form of participation in the Priesthood of Christ which does not derive its powers solely from the status of the baptised. The ministerial priesthood conforms to the features of the original call of the Twelve and the association of this apostolic office with the continuation of Christ's ministry to the baptised. It is in conformity with the objectivity of office that the priesthood is committed to the radical demands of Gospel discipleship and can be no less than a state of life. It is one of Balthasar's continuing gifts to the Catholic understanding of ministry that he is able to construct a consistent theology of the priesthood that embraces both a relational and a distinctive place within ecclesial relationships. Furthermore, he is able to offer a transcendent and personal horizon to the essentially immanent and communal dimensions of concrete pastoral life within the Church. Whether or not he has succeeded entirely in keeping these twin dimensions of spirituality together is not so important in the light of the fact that he is at least a theologian who has attempted this task. The *magisterium* has continually called the priesthood to the integration of the transcendent and immanent, the personal and the communal, but a theological and biblical justification for this insistence is of great importance to the penetration of such a vision into the praxis of priesthood and pastoral ministry. Balthasar certainly provides for this, and in spite of the limits of his ultimately transcendent approach it is possible to take up the main motifs of his theology of priesthood and relate them specifically to the most immanent and practical tasks of recovering a Christological identity for the priesthood that is personally liberating and pastorally fruitful.

We shall begin by outlining the basic theology of the Christian states of life in which Balthasar posits the ministerial priesthood. Here we will note the underlying complementarity and unity of the states of life which Balthasar sees as the context for appreciating any differentiation that might evolve at the secondary level of Ascesis and mission. As we move on to elucidating the specific characteristics of the priesthood as a state of life, we shall come to Balthasar's fundamental insight into the office of priesthood as having no other function than to serve the Church and to be the crystallisation of the love of Christ for his people. Finally we shall unpack what this might mean for the pastoral identity and mission of the ministerial priest in the concrete form of his life. How this corresponds to the spirit of the Evangelical Counsels and how priesthood is understood in this perspective as a life of consecration will be critically assessed in the light of the continuing self-understanding of the ministerial priesthood in its search to be a servant priesthood and a truly pastoral presence in the Church.

STATES OF LIFE WITHIN THE CHURCH: UNITY AND DIVERSITY

Balthasar's theology of the states of life within the Church, in their unity and diversity, is rooted in a profound ecclesiology of communion which allows each state of life to be perceived in its proper identity without being reduced to another gift or service, and at the same time affirming the fundamental relationship of the states to one another drawn into and completing the Body of Christ in mutual harmony and for the sake of the world. All Christian states of life, Balthasar makes clear, are necessary for the realisation of the Church's mission in the world. This profound sense of interdependence and harmony enables Balthasar to distinguish three states of Christian life: lay-married, priestly and those given to the Evangelical Counsels. The common denominator is the vocation of all to holiness, the vocation of all the baptised.

The lay state represents the Church's insertion into the world; the religious represents the interiority, the centre of love within the Church. Balthasar uses the image of the heart muscle to express this harmony. In the religious, the heart of the Church contracts to its centre, the contraction existing for the sake of the expansion, so that the life-giving blood can be transmitted to all parts of the body. His other image is that of the tree, which extends from its crown, down to its deepest roots. The broader the crown of the tree, the deeper must be its roots. The more radically the Church is rooted in the depths of love, symbolised by the Evangelical Counsels, the more fruitful her mission in the world, especially in the witness and mission of the laity.[2] The ministerial priesthood is understood by Balthasar to be in a 'medial' position and, as such, needs both to be rooted deeply in the life of the

---

2 Balthasar's rather idiosyncratic account of how the states of life interrelate is very clearly expressed by John O'Donnell, *The Mystery of the Triune God* (London: Heythrop, 1988).

Counsels and to be inserted into the heart of the world. This requires of the priesthood its own particular 'spirituality'.

The originality of Balthasar's vision and treatment of the states of Christian life lies in his ability to disclose simultaneously the complementarity and specificity of the states. In attending to the specificity of the states, it is important always to remember how, in Balthasar's perspective, they are dynamically co-ordinated with each other in the mystery of the Church's communion. To focus too finely and abstractly on the divisions of the states might lead to a perception of the states of holiness within Christian life that does not reach the sense of wholeness and unity that, for instance in *Lumen Gentium* is reflected as the dynamic of the call to holiness that builds up the unity of the Body of Christ. This sense of integration is not missing in Balthasar's original text, but that perhaps it is not sufficiently developed. This of course can be accounted for by the fact that Balthasar wrote much of this theology before the Second Vatican Council, and that indeed his insights into the unity of the Christian states of life did much to further the implications of this for the more developed vision of Vatican II

For Balthasar, the differentiation of states of life within the Church reveals essentially the concrete form that divine love takes in a broken and fragmented world. The weight of Balthasar's reflections inevitably falls on what he calls the state of election, a call given only to a few but for the sake of all. The state of election constitutes that of the religious life, a life lived explicitly according to the Evangelical Counsels and to the ministerial priesthood. By their very nature these twin states of election are representative in that they exist for the whole Church and for the holiness of all God's people. They do this in virtue of their witness to the presence and power of Christ and of the possibilities of a new creation in him, lost in the original sin of Adam but found again in the transforming love of Christ and the integration intended for us in paradise and accessible to us now again in the perfection of holiness.

Balthasar sees in the Evangelical Counsels the fullness of self-giving love that was possible in the state of integrity in paradise and is now reopened only on the Cross. The way back to paradise is by the way of the Cross and the complete abandonment of self that this entails. Paradise is now possible only under the form of renunciation. It is integration by way of the form of negation in order to complete the fullness offered to the whole Church. There are those who, like Christ, must empty themselves and not hold life as something to be grasped. This call to an intimate form of discipleship is, of course, common to all Christians but in the case of those called to election it takes on an objectivity, a rule which confronts the whole Church with the priority of Christ and of the demands of the Gospel.

Balthasar sees priesthood and religious life as two sides of a single election that have an inner dynamism towards each other. This dynamism towards each other is directed towards the Christian transformation of the world and it is in accordance with this premise that the Church as a whole must constantly deepen its own spirituality as well as the individual states of life.[3] It is clear, however, that Balthasar views this transformation in terms of separation from the world and a spirituality of transcendence. This is particularly true of the two complementary states of election, the priesthood and the religious life, whose engagement with the world sheds light away from themselves to focus only on Christ.

> Though they are in the world, they are called out of the world to take their stand by Christ and to represent him who is the alpha and omega of the world as a whole. They take their stand by Jesus Christ in order to complete with him his movement from the Father to the world. For this purpose, they have freed themselves from the 'spirit of the world' that they may be totally at the disposal of God's mission to the world in his Son. All the great Christian institutions in the world, in whatever way they have come into being, have been founded by persons who had first dedicated themselves wholly to the cause of Christ. This is true not only of the pioneering cultural activities of the monks in the transition from antiquity to the Middle Ages; it is a basic law even today. The more purely the transcendence, the other-worldliness, of the nature and message of Christ shines forth in the life of the messenger, the more deeply this nature and message will penetrate into the structures of the natural world.[4]

While it is evident that Balthasar is expressing the eschatological meaning of the Evangelical Counsels that is constantly affirmed in the self-understanding of religious orders and their specific commitment to the coming of the Kingdom, it is not so clear that he is representing as accurately the essence of what pastoral presence and mission means in the context of the ministerial priesthood. There is a sense of dualism that needs to be overcome, both in terms of theological categories and

---

3 *Christlicher Stand* (Einsiedeln: Johannes Verlag, 1977) ET *The Christian State of Life* (San Frnacisco: Ignatius Press, 1983) p. 348.
4 Ibid., p. 349.

in terms of pastoral praxis. Transcendence as such does not need to imply dualism, but needs to be expressed in the light of the demands that immanence makes in the incarnational horizons of Christian faith and mission. It is the specific immanent characteristics of priestly presence and ministry that the highly symbolic and abstract language of Balthasar cannot completely address. What he is able to focus for us, however, is the value of transcendence of eschatology and of radicalism as a necessary component to a full understanding of ministerial priesthood and its place within the transforming, Christological structure and dynamism of ecclesial reality.

This criticism, by recognising the limits in Balthasar's highly imaginative and original synthesis of the Christian states of life can also shed theological light on what may be described as a darkening landscape of the theology of the priesthood. What he brings out of a theological eclipse are structures for priestly identity and mission that are explicitly Christological and radically evangelical. They keep alive for ministerial priesthood the possibilities of the radicalism of the Gospel amidst the legitimate concerns that finding sociological and professional meaning have introduced to the spirituality and praxis of ministerial priesthood at this present time.

THE OBJECTIVITY OF PRIESTLY OFFICE AND THE SUBJECTIVE DIMENSIONS OF HOLINESS

We have seen that in Balthasar's theology the life of the priesthood and the life of the Counsels form one state of election. How Balthasar understands the inner connaturality between the priesthood and the Evangelical Counsels has to do with his understanding of the objectivity of the office of priesthood and what this asks in terms of the subjective surrender of the person. Balthasar is able to distinguish between the 'absoluteness of the objective ministry (*das Sein*)' and the 'absoluteness of the subjective commitment (*das Sollen*)'[5] of religious life. He contrasts the priest as one called primarily to office with the one chosen for the life of the Counsels as called to a personal following. Balthasar's description of this differentiation is highly nuanced and involves a particular kind of spiritual paradox that needs close attention if the reality it is seeking to express can be grasped.

5 Ibid., p. 372.

Those who have received the call of Christ under either aspect strive together, then, toward unity: One called to the priesthood is called primarily to the office, which then requires of him that he assimilate his whole person to that office; one chosen for the life of the counsels is called primarily to a personal following of the Son whose task it is to place his whole person at the disposal of and to submerge it in his official mission, and who requires of his followers that they do the same. Both the one called to the priesthood and the one called to, on the other hand, a work of that surpassing love that allows itself to be consumed as a holocaust for the world, the priest must depend on the evangelical state to hold this side of his office constantly before his eyes and in his memory. If Christians were perfect followers of Christ, the difference of emphasis would not be necessary: They would instinctively understand the unity of personal love and impersonal obedience. But since they are still 'foolish . . . and slow of heart to believe . . .' (Lk 25:25), the Lord, for their instruction, has placed the two representatives of the one call in contrasting positions so that each may see in the mirror of the other what is lacking in himself.[6]

Balthasar is expressing here the difference in kind and not in degree that the Second Vatican Council documents refer to when speaking of the distinctiveness of the ordained ministry. The Evangelical Counsels provide an intensification of the baptismal character of the holy people of God; religious life is understood primarily, therefore, as an expression of the priesthood of all the baptised. The subjective holiness (*das Sollen*) and the consecration of those in the Evangelical state is of a qualitatively different character than those in the ordained ministry whose pastoral office constitutes a particular form of participation in the Priesthood of Christ and his continuing service of the baptised. The holiness, therefore, of the Christian priest derives not from his baptismal character but from his ordained identity and from the subjective configuration with Christ that flows from this.

In particular it is the kenosis of Christ which, as we have seen, constitutes his eternal priesthood, and the sacrificial dimensions of his continuing priestly presence in the Church he loves as his own Bride and Body takes on the form of an official and public priesthood. In the way that religious orders refer to their original charisms which precede the juridical and structural ordering of their lives, so too the ministerial priesthood might refer to its original charism as the sacrifice

6 Ibid., pp. 372–3.

of the crucified one of himself that still is given for the life of the world through the ministry of the Church and in her ordained ministry who continue to speak and act *in persona Christi*. Being true to its origins as the crystallisation of the love of Christ for his Church the ministerial priesthood has no other function than to make itself disposable for this mission. How this touches the very being of the person called to that mission we have seen is at the heart of the Catholic doctrine of priestly character. How this touches the very being of the person called to personal holiness through appropriation to his mission is at the heart of the Catholic tradition of identifying priestly holiness with the spirit of the Evangelical Counsels. This is a strong element in Balthasar's insistence on the objectivity of office requiring the priesthood to be always perceived as a state of life and for him there is no other way that makes the ordained ministry credible.

THE MEDIAL POSITION OF PRIESTHOOD

A MEDIAL BUT RADICAL PLACE

Within the dynamic of the states of life the special ecclesial function of the ministerial priesthood and the subjective holiness and ministry of the state of the Counsels are completely integrated into the comprehensive priesthood of all the baptised. Through the relationship and interdependence of the states of life with one another, the priesthood of the baptised and the holiness of the whole body of Christ is drawn into its perfection. For Balthasar the ministerial priesthood moves not only between the lay and religious state, but at the intersection of Church and world. It has, Balthasar says, a medial position. This position of the priesthood between lay state and Evangelical state is evident, Balthasar argues, in the concrete form in which this state exists within the Church and in virtue of which it is able to participate in the other two states of life. In the Evangelical state the priest, through celibacy and obedience to the Bishop, shares to some extent in that separation from the world for the cause of Christ that characterises the religious life. Through the relative personal autonomy required by the demands of the pastoral vocation and by close involvement with the life of the parish, its orientation to family needs, to the formation of the laity and to a freedom regarding material possessions, the priest seems to have a kind of 'organic unity' with the lay state.

This medial position delineates the specific contours of the life and ministry of the ministerial priest and therefore carries with it its own inherent strengths and weaknesses. Balthasar understands this as precisely the *situs* of Christian asceticism in the life of a Christian priest and in his view the spirit of the Counsels take on a certain urgency if the priest is to hold together this medial position with its inevitable conflicts and enigmas.

As an image of spirituality the medial position of priesthood is not presupposed by Balthasar to be one that suggests a mediocrity. Rather, because the priesthood is inserted into the heart of the world by its position, its sense of disposal for mission requires a level of surrender that is wholly absorbing.

> This medial position of the priesthood has its advantages, but also its dangers: the advantage of immediate pastoral contact with the lay congregation; the even greater one of sharing with those in the evangelical state the privilege of a personal following of Christ. The priest can, in fact, assimilate his personal life as closely as he chooses to the spirit, and indeed to the reality, of the evangelical life. But there are also dangers attached to his medial position: The priest can fall prey to mediocrity and colorlessness, or even, in human weakness, extract from each way of life all that is pleasant in it while avoiding the radicality of 'losing his soul' (in marriage or in the evangelical state). Not that he must inevitably fall prey to these dangers; it was, after all, the Lord who placed the priesthood in this medial position by ordaining the difference between office and personal discipleship. It is for the priest to determine how far he will adapt his life to the office he has accepted and so allow the priesthood to become a genuinely medial state between the evangelical state and the lay state.[7]

The fact of the disparity between person and office becomes very concrete in the medial position of the ministerial priest. The need for an ever closer identity with the mission that has been entrusted becomes the means of personal consecration for the ministerial priest. It is essentially a pastoral asceticism and, as such, is experienced as a growing availability for mission. The Triune and Christological depths of this spirituality of personal identity and mission are inescapable and challenge the ministerial priesthood precisely because of its medial position to plunge ever more deeply into these depths, not only as doctrine, but as what constitutes life itself. It is perhaps in its doctrinal clarity that Balthasar's grasp of the relatedness of person and mission,

7 Ibid., p. 367.

office and personal holiness, the sacrifice of Christ and love for the world has most to offer to a contemporary spirituality of the ministerial priesthood as it seeks to find its place in the Church and in the world. The 'place' that Balthasar envisages, the medial position, is not only hierarchically constituted or structurally functional for service to the whole Church, but also is given as a gift of love by Christ to his Church. In allowing itself to be given and handed over, the priesthood loses itself to its identity as grace and not as a reality it can own or fashion for itself. In this lie the seeds of a servant spirituality and a holiness that is specifically and fundamentally pastoral.

PRIESTHOOD AND THE SPIRIT OF THE COUNSELS

In Balthasar's view it is the spirit and life of the Evangelical Counsels that guarantee the 'emptiness' within the priesthood for its full meaning of service and pastoral love to be realised. This form of emptying out is the Form of Christ, the state of life of Jesus himself in his Person and in his mission. It is in New Testament terms the 'having the mind that was in Christ Jesus'. Therefore, in connecting so closely the ministerial priesthood with the life of the Counsels, Balthasar is being radically biblical, and it is this radicalism that characterises his whole emphasis on the priesthood as a state of life. The state of life of the Christian priest, because it participates in the eternal priesthood of Christ and its continuation in the Church for the sake of all, is shaped within the obediential love, the poverty of kenosis and the chaste fruitfulness of the Son. These are transposed into modes of ministerial presence and pastoral love. They are what constitutes the transforming ministry of the Christian priest, and before a priest becomes part of the outreach of that transforming love, he must first allow himself to be drawn into its depths. The principle that is so evident to Balthasar, that interiority and mission are intrinsically woven together in Christ, operates no less when it comes to ministry in his name.

The spirit of the Counsels guarantees the radical reversal of authority and power that Jesus specifically refers to as the pattern of those who are called to leadership in the community. It is a pattern that completely undermines relationships of domination and control which have characterised every human society. The paradox of the institution and of the office of priesthood is precisely that it is to exemplify only the pattern of Christ who was sent as a servant.

(At the Last Supper) a dispute arose among them as to which one of them was to be regarded as the greatest. But Jesus said to them,

'The kings of the Gentiles lord it over them; and those in authority over them are called benefactors. But not so with you: rather the greatest among you must become like the youngest, and the leader like one who serves. For who is greater, the one who is at the table or the one who serves. Is it not the one at the table? But I am among you as one who serves' (Lk 22:24–7).

As men constrained by their Lord to a pattern of humility and service, those called to ministerial priesthood find the source of this self-renunciation in the living out of the spirit of the Counsels. Balthasar speaks of this as the humble obedience of the man who holds office becoming transparent to Christ only by completely losing himself and submitting his entire existence to the demands that this office brings. Balthasar is most stringent in his challenge to the priesthood that it should make this an existential law of its own life and self-understanding.

> The more he serves, accordingly, the better does the transparency succeed. The more he applies titles of dignity to himself, the more opaque does he become. Most of these titles contradict an explicit prohibition by the Lord. 'Father', 'pater', 'abbot', 'papa', and 'abbé' stand in opposition to Matthew 23:9; 'master' and 'magister' in opposition to Matthew 23:8; 'doctor' (in the ecclesiastical sense) in opposition to Matthew 23:10; 'lord' (*Dominus, Dom*) and 'my lord' (monsignore) in opposition to Luke 22:25; 'your Grace' (*euergetes*) likewise in opposition to Luke 22:25; and 'your excellency' and 'your eminence' in opposition to the instruction at Matthew 20:26–27; 23:11; Mark 9:35; 10:43–44; Luke 22:25; and John 13:13–17. Apart from the titles 'brother' and 'servant', which are permitted, at most only the title 'prelate' would come into question, since it expresses in material terms the office of presiding, but under the condition that every curate or chaplain would have a right to use it. How long – after the close of the feudal period, in which there were imperial and prince archbishops – will these obsolete and Christianly incomprehensible titles continue to be dragged along in the Church's baggage?[8]

Here, as elsewhere in Balthasar's writing on the priesthood, we are presented with a radical call towards a spirit of complete poverty in the sense of an utter dependence on faith that allows the priest to live

---

8 'Priesterliche Existenz', *Sponsa Verbi*, p. 396–397.

out of a sense of dependence on the power and presence of Christ, and not something less.

This 'something less' includes for Balthasar dependence on intra-ecclesial status, power and an over-reliance on ministerial skills and professional competence. Following Jesus requires the leaving of everything behind and the loss of self that the Gospel identifies with as the radicalism of the hidden treasure of the Kingdom for the sake of which all that he has '. . . must be sold'. For Balthasar it is the criterion of where the ultimate security of the priesthood lies that is the crucial test of its authenticity. To be truly authentic, the priesthood must make itself defenceless to the nakedness of faith and to the absolute demand of the Gospel. Before the Evangelical Counsels are juridical structures to enable and to order a life according to the Gospel, they are themselves a way of radically entering into the mystery of evangelical discipleship. It is to ensure such radicalism that Balthasar forcefully holds out this radical vision to the ministerial priesthood. It is certainly a different model of accountability than those which challenge the priesthood today to understand itself in terms of service and collaboration within the community of the Church. But it shares with this contemporary insight the recovery of a sense of spiritual renewal from which pastoral ministry can only grow more fruitful.

THE FEATURES OF OBEDIENCE, POVERTY AND CELIBACY IN PRIESTLY LIFE

We now turn our attention to the question as to how, more precisely, the threefold structure of the Evangelical Counsels direct and form the concrete shape of priestly spirituality. The Evangelical Counsels, which have come to be crystallised in the three fundamental features of Obedience, Poverty and Celibacy, are a form already distinctly recognisable in the Gospels (cf. e.g. Lk 9.37ff.; Mk 10.29ff.) and constitute the internal and dynamic principle which integrates the diverse pastoral dimensions of priestly life into the wholeness and holiness of office and person that each individual priest is asked to strive towards. The configuration to Christ through sacramental consecration defines the role and identity of the priest in the heart of the people of God, so that his participation in the pastoral and priestly office of Christ requires a gift of self that is at one and the same time both deeply personal and pastoral. To live the pastoral office as a total gift of self is fundamentally at the core of the Church's insistence on the continuing importance and relevance of the Evangelical Counsels to the vitality and apostolic fruitfulness of priestly ministry. Balthasar understands the chosenness and mission of the priest as the very condition which can offer the greatest possible chance of becoming a full person, of laying hold of his own substance, of grasping that most intimate idea of his own self, which, outside this radical sense of mission, would remain undiscoverable. Therefore the priest, as a 'theological person', is called to take a qualitative step into the specific form of those who are especially sent. Balthasar takes as an example of this the call of Peter, whose change of name from Simon expresses that he is no longer a private, empirical subject, but a person who has a new theological and social significance. This case illustrates for Balthasar the inner dramatic dimension of theological personhood, where man is not what he thinks himself to be but what God appoints him to be. He must apply all his strength to shift his personal centre into what is implied by the new theological name and its inevitable dimension of service of others. In the light of this analysis, the priest, in precisely forgetting his private subjectivity and becoming one with his function, grows into what is most distinctive and personal to him.

In this context, the Evangelical Counsels create the ethos of the kind of intense assimilation of identity to and in Christ which priestly configuration requires. In order to subjectively imitate that 'being for others' that characterises Christ's own mission, the Church lays upon the priesthood the objectivity of the Counsels, which as 'law' paradoxically draws the priest in his own frailty to fulfil its demands into the realms of pure grace. The features, therefore, of obedience, poverty and celibacy are essentially the contours of a life lived in total openness to a gift of holiness and ministerial fruitfulness that can only be given and not attained. The priest, therefore, receives the gift of his own self through the self-renunciation that is intrinsic to life according to the Counsels. The Church, too, receives life through the kenosis of her ministers, and it is at the level of both ecclesial and personal spirituality that the ministerial priesthood moves along its own journey of self-discovery and the fulfilment of its mission.

OBEDIENCE

At a certain level, obedience appears to be structured towards a mainly institutional and hierarchical dimension of ecclesial ministry. The priest, at his ordination, promises obedience to his Bishop and is publicly seen to be a man, radically available to the Church. There are structural elements of priestly obedience outlined clearly in canon law and the priest, as servant of the Church, is open to the pastoral contingencies and demands of the local Church as discerned by the Bishop and according to the judgements of ecclesiastical authority. The Holy Father, in *Pastores Dabo Vobis*, describes this hierarchical and institutional obedience, as one that is essentially apostolic. It entails an ecclesial generosity in which the priest gives himself over to the Church in such a way that he is assimilated entirely to its mission and outreach. The exercise of pastoral office can therefore never be diminished to what is merely subjective or convenient, but is always in reference to the building up of the Body. This requires, the Holy Father insists, a recognition and love of the Church in her hierarchical structure and the bond of unity with the Supreme Pontiff and the Episcopal College through a filial and obediential relationship with the diocesan Bishop as promised during the Rite of Ordination. As the Holy Father observes:

> This 'submission' to those invested with ecclesial authority is in no way a kind of humiliation. It flows instead from the responsible freedom of the priest who accepts not only the demands of an organized and organic ecclesial life, but also that grace of discernment and responsibility in ecclesial decisions which was assured by Jesus to his Apostles and their successors, for the sake of faithfully safeguarding the mystery of the Church and serving the structure of the Christian community along its common path towards salvation.[9]

The obedience asked of a priest becomes the foundation of his own authentic ministry of preaching and teaching: 'Only the person who knows how to obey in Christ is really able to require obedience from others in accordance with the Gospel.'[10] This aspect of the priest's obedience demands a marked spirit of asceticism in the letting go of personal preferences and points of view and in the collaboration with others that is a mark of the unity of the presbyterate. *Pastores Dabo Vobis* refers to this dimension of obedience as one that is communal and is one of solidarity expressed in a ministry of co-responsibility regarding directions to be taken and choices to be made.[11]

Finally, the Holy Father highlights the particular pastoral character of priestly obedience.

9 John Paul II, *Pastores Dabo Vobis, No. 28* (London: Catholic Truth Society, 1992), p.73.
10 Ibid.
11 Ibid., p. 74.

It is lived in an atmosphere of constant readiness to allow oneself to be taken up, as it were 'consumed', by the needs and demands of the flock. These last ought to be truly reasonable and at times they need to be evaluated and tested to see how genuine they are. But it is undeniable that the priest's life is fully 'taken up' by the hunger for the Gospel and for faith, hope and love for God and his mystery, a hunger which is more or less consciously present in the People of God entrusted to him.[12]

This is a view of priestly obedience echoed by Gisbert Greshake when he describes obedience in its biblical sense of self-offering and surrender, focusing on the witness of St Paul who understands himself as one whose life has been poured out in sacrificial service (Phil. 2.17), a holocaust for the Church.[13] The radical availability for mission in which the priest is to find his true freedom is therefore an obediential state of life that transcends the juridical structure and finds its origins in Christ's own obediential stance before His Father which constitutes the very heart of his own Priesthood.

Balthasar understands the official and somewhat impersonal mark of obediential ministry as the very condition within the priesthood that allows the personality of Christ to shine through with greater clarity. In fact, Balthasar places obedience at the very pivot of the efficacy of ecclesial ministry and in his view becomes the ethos of the priest where the gift of self is made most possible and where the office itself is able to succeed despite all human frailty and inadequacies.

The more unostentatiously the priest dedicates himself to his ministry in order to live only for it, the better he fulfils it. In such self-surrender, the priest 'loses his soul' – his subjectivity – in the act of obedience that is an essential part of every special election and mission. The authority represented and exercised by the ecclesial minister is that of Christ, the Redeemer, who was obedient unto death. It not only demands obedience; obedience is its very nature. Hence it cannot fail to incorporate more deeply into the obedience of Christ those on whom it is conferred. But it is not only authority *as* service; it is also, and explicitly, authority *for* service, for participation in the responsibility of the divine Shepherd who gives his life for his sheep (Jn 10:15) and who, in entrusting to others his pastoral love and responsibility, expects of the recipients that,

---

12 Ibid.
13 *The Meaning of Christian Priesthood* (Dublin: Four Courts Press, 1988), p. 135.

as 'he laid down his life for us', so they, too, will 'lay down [their lives] for the brethren' (I Jn 3:16).[14]

What *Pastores Dabo Vobis* describes in terms of apostolic, communal and pastoral, Balthasar speaks of in terms of the total expropriation of the priest's own private interests and inclinations so that he may be a pure instrument for the accomplishment of Christ's designs for the Church: 'In the priesthood, man is so completely a function that God can work in him even when he resists.'[15] Behind the stringent language, Balthasar is attempting to give expression, not only to the extent of the self-renunciation that is involved in the 'vow' of obedience, but to the radical and unrestricted extremes of love which is its source. The particular kind of readiness to accept the responsibilities of such an office has its roots in an interior disposition that allows itself to experience the self-emptying that is the model for all Christians of an authentic imitation of Christ. The concrete form of this self-emptying and obedience unto death is a life that the Church characterises as the Counsel of Poverty, the spirit of which in the life of the priest takes on the same apostolic, communal and pastoral nuance as in the case of the Counsel of Obedience.

POVERTY

The application of the Counsel of Poverty to the life and ministry of priests is explicitly a pastoral and apostolic one. In *Pastores Dabo Vobis* the Holy Father affirms that poverty ensures that priest remains available to be sent wherever his work will be most useful and needed, even at the cost of personal sacrifice. Quoting the Synod Fathers and the Council's teaching, he emphasises the image of Christ, who, 'rich as he was, became poor for love of us' (2 Cor. 8.9), as one which continues to guide the pastoral identity and ministry of priests and their witness to Christ through a simple lifestyle and a spirit of generous renunciation in material and worldly things.

As leader of the community the priest is, above all, to be honest and responsible in his administration of the goods of the community, committed to equitable distribution of goods among the presbyterate itself and a facilitator of a preferential option for the poor among the community and society at large. Here the Holy Father underlines the prophetic role of the priest in his proclamation of the Gospel to and

---

14 *Christlicher Stand*, p. 268.
15 Ibid., p. 274.

presence among those on the margins of society. This is an urgent task for the ministerial priesthood in the light of the tyranny of consumerist values in contemporary society. If the Christian priest as prophet is to witness to a new pattern of liberated life in Christ which refuses to become a slave to worldly things in its freedom for the values of the Kingdom, then he must first embrace these values in a life that strives towards the freedom of the Gospel. This prophetic role leads to a closer configuration with Christ who brings

> . . . his pastoral charity to perfection on the Cross with a complete exterior and interior emptying of self, (*which*) is both the model and source of the virtues of obedience, chastity and poverty which the priest is called to live out as an expression of his pastoral charity for his brothers and sisters. In accordance with Saint Paul's words to the Christians at Philippi, the priest should have 'the mind which was in Christ Jesus', emptying himself of his own 'self', so as to discover, in a charity which is obedient, chaste and poor, the royal road of union with God and unity with his brothers and sisters (cf. *Phil 2:5*).[16]

Balthasar likewise understands the spirit of poverty in terms of the Christological principles which interpret and fashion authentic ministerial priesthood. He recognises the essential ambiguity of the spirit of poverty in the context of what he terms the medial position of the priesthood. He is particularly sensitive to the inevitable administrative, practical and educational responsibilities that have accrued to the position of presbyter in the community. This development, for better or for worse, has brought the ministerial priesthood to its present stage of development within the community of the Church, and in so far as it has to occupy this 'medial' place, it is here that the priesthood encounters its own particular 'place' of asceticism and struggle with temptation. For Balthasar this includes the temptation to power, as opposed to the service that true authority entails and the temptation to evade the place of the cross in the soulless pursuit of programmes and structures that promise easy or utopian success. For Balthasar, the spirit of poverty drives the priest towards the total and absolute claims of the Gospel as the criterion of both his personal and professional existence and involves him in a process of self-emptying that is always 'for others'.

16 *Pastores Dabo Vobis* (London: Catholic Truth Society, 1992), p. 81.

Balthasar likes to highlight the quite painful experience of anonymity in which the basic disposition of sacrificing one's own individuality to a function that is itself and of its nature anonymous. 'Priests are, for the most part, interchangeable in the functions they perform.'[17] Balthasar insists that it can never be by the colossal proportions of individuality or even ideal self-image that the pastoral ministry reaches its fruition. It is by another way which is always the way of the Cross, which is a special form of humility that always takes in the form of personal life the attitude of a servant.[18]

A contemporary English parish priest and writer, Father Michael Hollings, suggests that the spirit of poverty in the ministerial priesthood is never more apparent than when the priest opens his heart, his door, his home and his life to those whom the Lord entrusts to him. Implicit in such a spirituality would be the generosity, hospitality and inherent simplicity that allows such pastoral availability to happen in the first place. At the very heart of the world, especially in its urban life, the priest living among his people enmeshed as they are in the ambiguous structures of the marketplace and the politic is in a medial place that is often itself impoverished at so many levels, both human and spiritual. As a faithful presence the priest experiences the beatitude of poverty in his pastoral asceticism of availability, service and love. Particularly where the religious landscape is one of huge indifference, if not positive rejection, the social structures no longer necessarily mirror to the priest a sense of his value or importance, and in this sense a social and cultural poverty as never before engages the priest in the everyday fabric of his personal and ministerial existence. It is here that Balthasar recognises a prophetic role for the priest, where his true source of energy and support is in the poverty of naked faith which becomes his only treasure and the powerlessness of the crucified one who becomes his wisdom and strength.

For Balthasar the spirit of poverty with all that it entails in terms of emptiness and openness for God and for others is intrinsically linked to the call to celibacy which does not make theological sense without its connectedness to the obediential self-emptying love of Christ to which ministerial priesthood is configured.

17 *Christlicher Stand*, p. 276.
18 Ibid.

CELIBACY

In the case of celibacy, once again the Church refers to its pastoral dimensions when applied to the life and ministry of priests. In *Pastores Dabo Vobis* configuration to Christ, the Head and Shepherd, involves a personal participation in the pastoral charity of Jesus Christ himself, 'a gift freely bestowed by the Holy Spirit and likewise a task and a call which demand a free and committed response on the part of the priest.'[19] The essential content of this pastoral charity is the gift of self, the total gift of self to the Church, following the example of Christ, 'who loved the Church and gave himself up for her' (Eph. 5:25). Quoting from an address given at the Eucharistic Congress in 1989, the Holy Father writes:

> Pastoral charity is the virtue by which we imitate Christ in his self-giving and service. It is not just what we do, but our gift of self, which manifests Christ's love for his flock. Pastoral charity determines our way of thinking and acting, our way of relating to people. It makes special demands on us . . .[20]

In this gift of self to the Church the priest is drawn into that love of the Church, both in its universal aspect and in that part of it that is entrusted to him, with a love analogous to the deep love of a husband for his wife. This gift of self has no limits and is marked by 'the same apostolic and missionary zeal of Christ the Good Shepherd'.[21] In this way the primary point of reference of the priest's ministry is Christ himself, whose charity becomes 'a source, criterion, measure and impetus for the priest's love and service to the Church, the Body and Spouse of Christ'.[22] It is this principle of pastoral charity which unifies the many activities of the priest and is the essential unity of his life and mission. It is the fundamental option of his life 'to give his life for the flock', and existentially to assume the role of the Good Shepherd.[23]

It is for this reason that *Pastores Dabo Vobis* strongly affirms the tradition in the Western Church to maintain, despite all difficulties and objections, the link between celibacy and sacred ordination. While recognising that celibacy is a law of the Church which is open to

19 *Pastores Dabo Vobis*, p. 58.
20 Ibid.
21 Ibid., p. 59.
22 Ibid.
23 Ibid., p. 61.

development and diversity as in the case of the discipline of the Oriental Churches, the thrust of its position is towards clarifying the theological motivation for celibacy and its place within ecclesial spirituality. Therefore the Holy Father emphasises celibacy as an experience that 'ought not to be considered and lived as an isolated or purely negative element, but as one aspect of a positive, specific and characteristic approach to being a priest.'[24]

Celibacy is therefore understood as a positive enrichment of the priesthood, as a gift given by God to the Church, and as a sign of the Kingdom which is not yet of this world and is still to come As with obedience and poverty, the pastoral dimension is highlighted, not in any extrinsic sense, as if the priest simply had more time or energy for working for the Kingdom, but as a qualitative stance towards God and others. In this sense celibacy is not merely a practical arrangement to allow for more pastoral availability, but rather a mystical or spiritual state of life.

In Balthasar's reflections on priestly life, celibacy is similarly understood to be a personal identification and consecration to Christ that is asked for by the nature of the priestly office itself. The juridical law of celibacy institutionalises the radical call of leaving all things to follow on the path that the Son has already taken. Balthasar in many passages gives expression to this principle of discipleship as one that asks the one called to go far beyond the natural capacities and limits of what can reasonably be asked. The fruitfulness that emerges from what seems a 'dying' is an intrinsic part of the paradox of the Christian mystery of crucified life and love. All of Balthasar's ecclesial thinking as we have seen circles around the original Christian community of love gathered around the Cross and the profound symbolism of Mary and John. In these twin figures the paradox of Christian virginity unfolds at its starkest point of where life is overwhelmed by death and where the possibility of a new creation is solely in God's power and providence. Priestly celibacy can only be correctly understood when seen in the light of what appears to be at first glance life-denying and without hope for a future and the natural fruitfulness for which human destiny holds out.

In Balthasar's view attempting an *apologia* for a celibate priesthood is as uncomfortable as searching for one that justifies the folly of contemplative existence.[25] The practical or empirical evidence for the

---

24 Ibid., p. 77.
25 Hans Urs von Balthasar, *Sponsa Verbi* (Einsiedeln: Johannes Verlag, 1961), pp. 28–29.

fruitfulness of these lives may not be as apparent as the rather more optimistic and rigorous voices in their defence tend to infer. Balthasar takes very seriously the darkening horizon of religious consciousness, particularly in the Western Church, and tends to view the future as one in which fewer people will be able to live the radicalism and aloneness of this Counsel. Yet here he sees an apocalyptic moment for the Church in which its primal hunger and thirst for the presence and power of the perfection of the Evangelical Counsels will perhaps resurrect a sense of feasting from its profoundly life-giving depths in the very heart of the painful experience of what he describes as a time of famine.

It is this note of joy and the fullness of life that pervades much of what Balthasar actually writes about the validity of the Evangelical Counsels and their appropriate meaning for the priestly state of life. While Balthasar does not deny the dimensions of celibacy that support a greater availability to others, he tends to focus more on the interiority that is involved. In keeping with his theological method and its fundamental Trinitarian concern, Balthasar understands the individual, the solitary as always in communion with others through the communion of the Blessed Trinity. In fact it is only through the interpersonal and Trinitarian relationships of life and love that the Christian disciple or priest is actually fashioned into an individual person. Jesus himself is a person because of the Father and in relation to Him; he is a person because the Father has sent him in the upholding love and fellowship of the Holy Spirit.

Balthasar, in a moving passage towards the end of the third volume of *Theodrama*, in the section headed 'The Individual', meditates on the 'celibacy' of the Son at the moment of his apparent forsakenness:

> In John we read these solemn words: 'The hour is coming, indeed it has come, when you will be scattered, every man to his home, and will leave me alone; yet I am not alone, for the Father is with me' (Jn 16:32). Nor is this Johannine expression in conflict with the Markan and Matthean cry of dereliction on the part of Jesus on the Cross. The experience of utter forsakeness is an integral part of the Son's mission; it remains a form of the closest relationship, even when it appears in the mode of God's turning away from him. And it is precisely in this relationship of forsakeness that the solitary, isolated Son exercises the most fruitful phase of his apostolate. For it is now that he gives birth to the Church. Christian fruitfulness, which takes place in solitude (even to the extent of forsakeness), cannot be experienced by the one who thus bears fruit. It takes place

within a trinitarian fellowship that, as far as subjective experience is concerned, vanishes into nothing at the boundary; objectively, however, it is never more effective than then.[26]

The relocation, then, of the meaning of celibacy within the context of priesthood to its origins in Trinitarian and crucified love is, for Balthasar, the only means of freeing it from the polemics of debate and the contingencies of the present crisis of numbers and of morale. There is no more radical way of viewing celibacy than in terms of fruitfulness and its mysterious character in Christian revelation. That this character may at times appear to be paradoxical,[27] foolish,[28] forsaken,[29] powerless,[30] or fragile[31] is in Balthasar's view entirely consistent with Christian origins and the form of Christ and its realisation through the passionate engagement of God with the world. Sharing in this passionate involvement of God is the meaning of priestly ministry, and celibacy, in Balthasar's vision, can be a powerful sign and promise of precisely this passion and the urgency and power it brings.

CONCLUSION

It will have become clear that Balthasar's understanding of the priesthood as a state of life rests on his fundamental grasp of the wholeness of ecclesial consciousness that allows for an almost complete connectedness between the mysteries of faith, especially those Trinitarian and Christological, with every detail and structure of Christian and ecclesial living. For him there is an unambiguous connaturality between the objective office of the ministerial priesthood and the radical and subjective demands of a life of intense discipleship as enshrined both canonically and spiritually in the Evangelical Counsels.

The capacity to contain what has become in practice a fragmented and painful dimension of the Church's life and mission in a beautifully fashioned synthesis of doctrine and spirituality, clearly defined in contours of identity and commitment, might appear to some as a failure to grasp the grey areas of the theology of priesthood and the contemporary questions surrounding its authentic shape and identity

26 Hans Urs von Balthasar, *Theodramatik*, vol. III, pp. 450f.
27 Ibid.
28 Ibid.
29 Ibid.
30 Ibid.
31 Ibid.

which certainly dominate the contemporary literature. In particular, the limits of Balthasar's own experience as a priest rooted in a profound sense of community with all of its Johannine characteristics of interior and abiding love need to be taken into account in the light of the realities that face ministerial priests who do not belong to religious congregations and whose spirituality is essentially pastoral and in Balthasar's own language, ambiguously medial. How the ministerial priesthood is to adapt to its changing circumstances and to the changing Church and world of which it finds itself a part, is a question and an agenda which Balthasar does not address directly. It might be justifiably argued that his theological sensibilities kept him at a distance from this issue in so far as his theological style and method tends towards the ideal and transcendent vistas of theological reflection.

This distance becomes apparent when compared with contemporary insights into the dimensions of discipleship and ministry that are transforming for society and the world in all its socio-political realities. The intrinsic link of the Evangelical Counsels with the values of the Kingdom and their realisation through a lifestyle that is often countercultural is an emphasis that Balthasar, while not negating it, would not highlight. Participation in the transformation of the world as a constitutive dimension of the preaching of the Gospel is a form of ministry that Balthasar would see as in need of continual baptism into the paradox of the Paschal mystery which for him defied any social or political equation. The search for utopia is for Balthasar a constant temptation for the Church, whose place in the world is not guaranteed to be anything other than the place of the Cross. All pastoral planning and programmes for the coming of the Kingdom into the world, in Balthasar's view, can never by-pass the criterion and the crisis of the Cross.

It is essential to understand, then, both the limits and the contribution of Balthasar's spirituality of the ministerial priesthood. He does not offer a pragmatic account of how priesthood is to structure itself around the values and realisation of the Kingdom nor how it is to enter into a transforming and liberative pastoral praxis. What he does offer is the content, the inner form from which such a praxis can unfold. At one level his account of the priestly state of life, with its obvious antecedents in the French School of spirituality and the teaching of Pierre de Bérulle, is highly individualistic, mystical and monastic. In marked contrast to contemporary trends in priestly spirituality, we find in Balthasar's writings a creative and radical recasting of these classical traditions. They do not certainly represent the whole range of images and models of priestly presence and ministry, yet they have their place and need to be integrated into the more communal, functional and collaborative paradigms of priestly ministry that pervades the contemporary scene.

As to the possibility that a celibate presbyterate and a married presbyterate might be understood as theologically equal options, Balthasar himself viewed the model of the *vir probatus* as an exception to the rule and as an experience in the Church that would lead ultimately to a more positive re-evaluation of the evident rightness and indispensability of celibacy as a form of life in the Church. The compatibility of the two sacraments of marriage and priesthood as understood by a writer such as Heinz-J. Vogels, who refers the self-giving love of a husband and father of a family to its origins in Christ's own love for his Church and who recalls the teaching of the letter to Timothy in comparing the duties of a father of a family and a pastor, is a view of an integration of the states of life that would not be consistent with Balthasar's more abstract and delineating approach.[32] It is clear that Balthasar's stylised treatment of the states of life was not carried on in dialogue with the more affirming and positive accounts of personal and especially conjugal relationships which are a characteristic of post-Conciliar Catholic thinking. In no sense could Balthasar be described as negative towards marriage or human intimacy. Indeed his writings convey a deep sensitivity to the depths of love and commitment and a grasp of the dimensions of sacrificial love to which Christian marriage aspires. Yet as we have seen in other areas of his theology, Balthasar can seem to be at a distance from the full reality, practical concerns and social and economic factors that theology needs to address and embrace.

This weakness, however, does not diminish the power of his spiritual insight into the radicalism of Christian holiness and of priestly existence. The absence of the pragmatic, in a sense, allows us to face the level of the very being of the priest as person. Balthasar plunges reflection on the priesthood into the recently uncharted waters of the objectivity of office, the ontology of priestly identity and the hiddenness of grace. In this he brings both depth and theological imagination to a ministry that is conscious of its function, but in crisis over its identity. It is precisely as a spirituality that seeks to integrate function and personal identity that Balthasar's vision has a concrete contribution to make to the presence and ministry of priests in the Church and in the world.

---

32 Heinz-J. Vogels, *Celibacy – Gift or Law?* (Tunbridge Wells, Kent: Burns & Oates/ Search Press, 1992).

VI

THE MINISTERIAL PRIESTHOOD: ITS CLASSICAL MODES OF MINISTRY AND PRESENCE WITHIN THE CHURCH

POINTERS TO A SPIRITUALITY: THE CONCRETE FORM OF PRIESTLY LIFE AND MINISTRY

One of the guiding principles of Balthasar's Christological method is that of the concrete universality of the love of God which chooses incarnation and crucifixion as its means of remaining present in the world. Jesus Christ is therefore the concrete Form within which the universal fullness of the love of God comes to expression, not as an idea but as the community of the Church, the concretely determined Form of the universal love of God in Christ translated into the social and historical dimension. Balthasar perceives here, precisely in the very concrete structures of the Church in the world, the tangible expression and proof of Triune love which ultimately integrates and gives meaning to the often all too human and fragmented aspects of institutional frailty.

'Ecclesiastical concreteness' therefore does not restrict Christian and ecclesial spirituality, but rather grounds it in the boundless possibilities of divine involvement which, as love, comes to the fore more starkly in the vulnerability of the institutional Church than in the sphere of the world which does not yet know the intimacy of the love which is in fact its origin and its fulfilment. The ministerial priesthood takes its Form within this sphere and shares in the twofold transcendence of Christ and his Church, towards the Father and for the sake of the Father's love, towards the world.

In Catholic life and tradition this has come to be closely identified with the ministerial priesthood, who in the local Church are called to live out concretely and existentially the mystery of incarnate and redemptive love, after the pattern of the Good Shepherd who lays down his life for his sheep. Balthasar's spiritual theology of Church and of mission, stamped as it is by this concept of the concrete Form of Christ, is especially suited to the specific area of the spirituality of the priesthood and the concrete, pastoral demands of its medial place both in the Church and in the world.

In this chapter we shall look at the classical functions of the ministerial priest, exploring how as Shepherd, President, Teacher, Reconciler, and Prophet, the priest is intimately linked to the mysteries of the Lord's own ministry and mission.[1] In the light of Balthasar's spiritual theology, the spiritual journey of the priest becomes the way of kenosis and the way of humble presence. The charism of the priest in his pastoral office is that through his presence with and to his people, he witnesses to the original presence of the Incarnate God who from all eternity wills Himself to be Emmanuel, God with Us. The Incarnation in its redemptive aspect is at the centre of the pastoral vocation of the diocesan priest: the gift of Balthasar's methodology is that it allows ecclesial ministry to see more clearly the contours of the Incarnate Lord in the shape and concrete form of ordinary Christian existence and ministry.

PRIESTLY PRESENCE: THE NEARNESS OF GOD TO HIS PEOPLE

When we apply the principles of Balthasar's Christological methodology to the specific concerns of a spirituality of the ministerial priesthood, it is primarily the Incarnational thrust of Balthasar's method that emerges as so appropriate to the task. According to Balthasar the Christian affirmation that God is with us unfolds from the most profound sense of the divine involvement that is at once intimately personal and publicly 'for all'. The whole identity of the pastor in Catholic tradition is connected to a fundamental incarnational grasp of ecclesial life, in which the statement 'God is with us' is first a proclamation of a living experience of God and the communion of life that shapes and sustains this experience. The pastor proclaims in his own life and ministry within the community of faith the Incarnation of God. The whole etymology of the concept of the priest within his

1 Cf., J. Colson, *Ministre de Jésus-Christ ou le Sacerdoce de l'Évangile* (Paris: Editions du Cerf, 1966), and G. Martelet, *Deux Mille Ans d'Église en Question* (Paris: Editions du Cerf, Vol 1, 1984, Vols. 2 and 3, 1990).

diocese and local community of faith seeks to focus this truth. The word 'diocesan' comes from the Greek *dioikein*, which means 'to keep house' or 'to manage a household'. In each diocese the care of the Bishop for his spiritual household is extended to the parish level. The word 'parish' comes from the Greek word *paroikos*, which means 'dwelling beside or near'.[2]

The presence, therefore, of the priest in his parish is as a witness to the fundamental presence of God's care: God's 'dwelling beside or near', the 'ordinary and commonplace household' of His people is witnessed to in the pastoral vocation of the diocesan priest who is called to live near the community entrusted to his care. The sense of 'living beside' and sharing life with the people of God roots the servant priesthood in the most radical and concrete experience of incarnational and redemptive mission. The radical witness, therefore, of the priest of the parish rests in Christ's call to root priestly presence in the very fabric of the commonplace, everyday life of the people. It is Balthasar's consistent linking together of the themes of Incarnation, Mission and Church that provides the priesthood with the theological synthesis that enables it to grasp more fully its unique calling to live an incarnational life, to remain near the people, yet be continually open to a mission that is beyond simple maintenance of community life and order.

Living beside or near his people, the priest lives out of the whole mission of the Son: he is called to walk on the way the Son has already gone, and of so walking with his people that the fullness of Triune love opens up not as an extrinsic demand, but as the connatural condition of the possibilities of the *communio* that has allowed for this relationship in the first place. It is in the fabric of the ordinary moments and experience of human life that the transformation takes place: it is in the Catholic grasp of the 'wholeness' of this experience that the sacramental and social aspects of the life of the parish community are seen in their fundamental mutuality, expressions of the one *agape* that brings together into unity the diversity of ecclesial functions and life.

The notion of the 'whole' as fragment which is so essential to Balthasar's theology of ecclesial relations opens up a vision for the local and ordinary *diakonia* of the parish community that does not place mission and maintenance in opposition, but as interrelated and mutually supportive. John Paul II, in his Apostolic Exhortation, *Pastores Dabo Vobis*, recalls the mission of the priest to its roots in the mystery of the Church as a communion of love and affirms the fundamentally

2 Cf. Paul T. Keyes, *Pastoral Presence and the Diocesan Priest* (Whittinsville, Mass.: Affirmation House, 1978).

'relational' dimensions of community and mission in Catholic ecclesial self-understanding. The Holy Father writes:

> The Apostolic Exhortation *Christifideles laici*, summarizing the Council's teaching, presents the Church as mystery, communion and mission: 'She is mystery because the very life and love of the Father, Son and Holy Spirit are the gift gratuitously offered to all those who are born of water and the Spirit (cf. Jn 3.5), and called to relive the very *communion* of God and to manifest it and communicate it in history (mission)'.
>
> It is within the Church's mystery, as a mystery of Trinitarian communion in missionary tension, that every Christian identity is revealed, and likewise the specific identity of the priest and his ministry. Indeed, the priest, by virtue of the consecration which he receives in the Sacrament of Orders, is sent forth by the Father through the mediatorship of Jesus Christ, to whom he is configured in a special way as Head and Shepherd of his people, in order to live and work by the power of the Holy Spirit in service of the Church and for the salvation of the world.
>
> In this way the fundamentally 'relational' dimension of priestly identity can be understood.[3]

Ministerial priests are called to prolong the presence of Christ, the one High Priest, by making him visible in the midst of the flock entrusted to their care. Consequently the nature and mission of the priesthood is defined through the interconnection of relationships which constitute the communion of the Church. The mutual immanence of the priest and his people is a representation of the mystery of the Church as essentially related to Jesus Christ. In Balthasar's ecclesial vision she is Christ's fullness, his Body, his Bride: the essential Marian and nuptial mystery which is at the deepest level of the consciousness of the Church has the priesthood totally at its service.

The diocesan priesthood, particularly when it is clearly 'local' and 'near', stands beside the Marian mystery as foster-father of the life of Christ that is brought forth by the mother Church into the world. Dwelling beside the Church of Christ, the priest is caught up in the incarnate, human and holy economy of life which he can never possess for himself in so far as he is merely the steward of these mysteries.

3 John Paul II, *Pastores Dabo Vobis, No. 12* (London: Catholic Truth Society, 1992), p.34.

His task of building up the Body of Christ, of shepherding God's people and of actuating the Church's sacramental signs of the presence of the risen Christ is proclaimed by the preface of the liturgy of the Chrism Mass, a special moment for priests when each year in the midst of their people and in the presence of their Bishop they pray for a renewal of their priestly existence.

By your Holy Spirit you anointed your only Son High Priest of the new and eternal Covenant. With wisdom and love you have planned that this one priesthood should continue in the Church. Christ gives the dignity of a royal priesthood to the people he has made his own. From these, with a brother's love, he chooses men to share his sacred ministry by the laying on of hands. He appointed them to renew in his name the sacrifice of redemption as they set before your family his paschal meal. He calls them to lead your holy people in love, nourish them by your word, and strengthen them through the sacraments. Father, they are to give their lives in your service and for the salvation of your people as they strive to grow in the likeness of Christ and honour you by their courageous witness of faith and love.[4]

Bringing this vision to life in the ordinary ministry of the priest requires a spirituality that is rooted in Triune and incarnate faith: it is precisely in this task that Balthasar's theological synthesis has a significant contribution to make.

THE PRIEST AS PRESIDENT: CELEBRATING THE SACRED MYSTERIES

For Balthasar, the celebration of the liturgy, especially the Eucharist, is the gathering of the worshipping community for the worship of the Triune God and nothing less. If this perception fades, the inclination he believes is for the community to celebrate itself. The gift of the ministerial priesthood to the Church is that it safeguards the community from understanding liturgy as merely a self-actualising celebration. The priest as President of the Eucharistic Assembly stands *in persona Christi*, the head of his Body the Church, the Bridegroom for whose coming the Church as Bride awaits. In Balthasar's view the

4 Preface to the Chrism Mass, *The Roman Missal.*

priesthood is the crystallisation of the love of Christ for his Bride and his Body; in this perception Balthasar stands within the tradition that sees the priest as essentially the icon of Christ. This is not to be conceived in any static sense, but as intrinsic to the dynamic of the divine initiative which makes liturgy possible and which understands the Lord's presence as gift. The spirituality of the iconic nature of priesthood gives expression to the profoundly biblical and patristic image of Christ the Bridegroom, clothed in his glory, coming to his Church who in bridal love now waits in joyful hope. The proclamation of this hope is the essential *mysterium fidei*, founded in the crucible of the Lord's Passion and the fruit of his crucified love, and accessible in the present through the power of the risen Lord and through the action of the Holy Spirit. The function of the President is to represent the initiating and transcendent self-giving of Christ who himself bestows on the community what it cannot by its own spiritual energies achieve. What we receive comes before what we do. In other words, the horizontal dimension of fellowship depends on the vertical and can only be understood authentically on that basis.

The priest is not only identified by his liturgical function, but is defined by it. His whole existence is given over to the sacred task of representing Christ, the head and spouse of the Body. The Second Vatican Council speaks of the union of the priest with Christ as coming to its clearest expression in the celebration of the liturgy.

> The purpose then for which priests are consecrated by God through the ministry of the bishop is that they should be made sharers in a special way in Christ's priesthood and, by carrying out sacred functions, act as his ministers who through his Spirit continually exercises his priestly function for our benefit in the liturgy ... Therefore the eucharistic celebration is the centre of the assembly of the faithful over which the priest presides. Hence priests teach the faithful to offer the divine victim to God the Father in the sacrifice of the mass and with the victim make an offering of their whole life.[5]

It is evident from Balthasar's theology of ecclesial identity that the priest is called by the very public and official obligations of his ecclesial office to appropriate existentially and spiritually the attitude of Christ himself in his obediential self-offering to the Father. In showing the

---

5 *Presbyterorum Ordinis*, ed. A. Flannery OP (Collegeville: Liturgical Press, 1978), n. 5.

depth of his love, Jesus the priest proclaims, takes, blesses, breaks and gives the bread; in the Breaking of the Bread the priest is called to bring his own being, his very self, into the sacred offering he is set apart to sacrifice.

Both Balthasar and Bouyer speak movingly of the priest coming to so identifying himself with the Eucharistic self-donation of Jesus that he comes to love the community entrusted to him as somehow his own body, his bride.[6] It is an intimacy which does not intrude into the Lord's unique bond of love with his Church, but rather through the mystery of participation is itself part of the gift and the fruit of that love. Priestly mediation does not eclipse the divine involvement but is the foundation of the possibility of the full encounter of love between Christ and his Church. In Catholic tradition the priesthood is willed by Christ himself and is an intrinsic dimension to the disclosure in liturgy and in life of how much He 'is love'.

In the context of the ordinary parish community this vision of the priestly presidential role serves a twofold purpose: in the first place, it saves the community from being simply a group of like-minded people, closed in on their own self-actualising experience. Eucharist is not a self-actualising process; it is a gift and it is a coming. In the second place, it lifts people and priests out of themselves into a communion that is the whole Church, the communion of saints and into the future that is the coming of God's Kingdom. Hereto the local church finds within its centre a sacred space for the world that is no longer out there, but is embraced in Triune love. The pastor, as President, is called not only to decrease so as to let Christ increase, but to lead the community in becoming less its own centre and finding its centre in Christ, and through him, with him and in him the abyss of Triune love for the world.

Rather than inhibiting the function of the diocesan priest in his sacramental ministry to only a cultic and symbolic figure, this spirituality opens up the consciousness of priestly liturgical prayer and presence into one that is fully ecclesial, and for that reason open to the world and to the imminence of the Kingdom. It also has the value of heightening the responsibility of the President for enabling and calling forth from the priestly people the richness and diversity of ministry which in the liturgical renewal has come to be seen as truly collaborative. An iconic spiritual theology of the priesthood need not be seen as undermining the priestly calling of the whole people of God, but as its very foundation

6 See above, Chapter III, on the essential Marian, feminine character of the Church and the masculine principle of Office.

and guarantee. The space and context created by the President and
entered into by the assembly needs to embrace a content that will be
transforming and sacramental. A community needs to be in touch with
its own dynamic and consciousness and it is the pastoral priesthood in
the midst of the people of God which is called to facilitate and enable
this journey of faith and of praise to take place in word and in symbol,
in time and in place. As Dom Basil Pennington has written of the vital
role of the President:

> All of this places a new responsibility on the presiding priest. There,
> within the celebration, he will have to be sensitive and capture the
> movement of the particular assembly so that he can most effectively
> call them forth from their present experience to the fullest
> participation in the great prayer, to the livelier sense of oneness with
> the celebrations of heaven. It is here where the eternal fullness of
> redemptive love is brought into the here and now of a particular
> Christian community and made relevant.[7]

Such a dynamic understanding of the role of President as mediator
demands at the same time the most personal appropriation of the
liturgical function. Pennington continues:

> A priest cannot limit himself to being a priest-mediator only when
> he is standing at the altar: he must be so in the fabric of his
> consecrated being. He is a man taken from among men for this.
> The mass is the high point of his mediatorial activity. But his whole
> life is to be one of mediation. His words of counsel and his presence
> are to be a constant mediation of God's love, and a receiving of his
> people and their love, joy, sorrows and pain for the Father. It is
> only in the context of a full attitude and life of mediation that a
> priest can truly pray his priestly prayer at the mass in a way that
> will call forth from the people a whole-hearted, empowered Amen.[8]

For the ministerial priest this role of mediation takes him like his
master outside of the holy place so that the whole world might be
sanctified in Christ. Precisely because of this, the priest's pastoral love
flows from the celebration of the Eucharist and finds there its highest
realisation. It is from the Eucharist that he receives the capacity to give

7 Basil Pennington, *The Eucharist Yesterday and Today* (Slough: St Paul Publications,
1984), p. 38.
8 Ibid., p. 57.

to his whole life and ministry a sacrificial dimension which becomes the inner principle of all his external activities and the demands of a socio-cultural context that is strongly marked by complexity and fragmentation. In his life the diocesan priest is called to radiate the spousal character of love which, celebrated in the Sacred Mysteries, becomes the source of truly loving God's people in the constant and faithful dedication of pastoral responsibilities and the cares of the community.

PRIEST AS TEACHER AND AS PROPHET

In Balthasar is to be found a very definite and clear sense of the primacy and authority of the Word of God in the life of priests who are called to be ministers of the Gospel. In this he reflects the teaching of *Presbyterorum Ordinis* which affirms:

> . . . that it is the first task of priests as co-workers of the Bishops to preach the Gospel of God to all men. In this way they carry out the Lord's command: 'Go out into the whole world and preach the Gospel to every creature' (Mark 16.15) . . . Priests then owe it to everybody to share with them the truth of the Gospel in which they rejoice in the Lord. Therefore whether by having their conversation heard among the Gentiles they lead people to glorify God; or by openly preaching proclaim the mystery of Christ to unbelievers; or teach the Christian message or explain the Church's doctrine; or endeavour to treat of contemporary problems in the light of Christ's teaching – in every case their role is to teach not their own wisdom, but the Word of God and to issue an urgent invitation to all men to conversion and to holiness.[9]

According to Balthasar, the Gospel is 'Glad Tidings' in so far as it is the Word not of the minister, but of God Himself. The priest is one who imparts the wisdom of another: dispensing and breaking open the word of life to others, the priest cannot alter or diminish its content or power. This absolute authority and primacy of the Word becomes the cutting edge for the ascesis of its authentic proclamation. In his preaching and catechesis the priest constantly surrenders himself to the wisdom and light that is not his own: like Jesus the Teacher 'he comes not to do his own will, but the will of the one who sends him.'

9 *Presbyterorum Ordinis*, n.4.

At this level of spiritual consciousness, Balthasar brings the specific challenge to the pastoral priesthood of the radical call to be obedient. For inasmuch as priests are called to proclaim the word in both the witness of what they say and in what they do, they must first in Balthasar's view become hearers of the word. They are to cultivate a listening heart.

Spirituality as a process is not a linear one, but an unfolding of a pattern of life that integrates vision and action, contemplation and service, ministry and life. The willingness to live like this is far deeper than the appropriation of ministerial skills; it has to do with a surrender of the whole self, to become what we are in Jesus Christ. Priests in their pastoral vocation are to draw energy and direction in and from Christ to build up the community of faith and to transform the world in the light and values of the Gospel. In this sense the Word of God truly becomes a two-edged sword. For Balthasar this is experienced in ministry as a challenge to move off the comfortable middle ground of self-analysis and ideological polarities to the place where the Word continues to gather the Church and to be proclaimed, the place of the Cross. Here the priest searching for prophetic authenticity and solidarity with the world is saved from himself and is set free to be with and to be for others. Like the prophets of the Old Testament who taught Israel to walk on ways that would lead to the future with God, priests in their role as prophetic teachers must first learn to walk with and to follow Jesus, to listen to his Word. These lessons of discipleship challenge the priest to face the absolute demands of the truth of the Gospel and to the radical demands of the responsibilities of office. Jesus Christ is himself the Gospel and is himself the essence of the Good News.

Balthasar believes that the primacy of Jesus in the structures of the Church needs to be constantly reaffirmed if the Church is not to depend merely on the contingency of social and personal relationships that do not last. The Church's prophetic task must include first a constant subjecting of herself to the light of the judgement of Christ, to make her structures as far as possible transparent to Christian love, so that the Church as a whole may witness more fully to God's action in the world. He writes:

Of this nature are structures such as the sacraments, holy Scripture, and also, of course, the ordained ministry. But as these crystallizations of the divine love are manifested in the sphere of the temporal and used by sinful men who also place their own interpretation on their meaning, so these structures also fall within the sphere of man's capacity to misuse them and to change their meaning. They therefore need to feel the breath of the authentic spirit of Christian love blowing through them in order to be credible. Throughout the centuries, Christians-priests as well as layman (sic) – fall prey to the temptation to endow isolated structures, authorities, and institutions with the quality of the sacred, and in doing this they inevitably call forth protests from the Church and invite revolution and open confrontation. It is none the less still possible to maintain that the structures of the Church are more easily permeated than those of the world, however convinced one may be, on sociological grounds, that the contrary is true (for example, with regard to the priesthood today). The structures of the Church already contain something of the quality of the New Age, and one cannot say that they will not attain fulfilment in the risen life to come.[10]

To be able to live with the truth, the priest as teacher and as prophet must not try to escape the weight of this responsibility by finding new and exciting methods of Christian engagement with the world which might subtly attempt to dilute the content of revelation. In the obvious lyricism of Balthasar's approach there is a real grasp of the issues at stake in what we continue to say and to do about Christian priesthood. His challenge to our response is whether contemporary paradigms will lead to a retreat from the radicalism of the Gospel and the weight of tradition or whether priesthood can remain true to its origins in the Word and the Wisdom of the Cross which often appears as 'foolish' to the world. The priest as Teacher needs to find the courage to be a prophet. He finds this as a power that belongs to the whole Church stronger than all his own initiatives and skills, yet accessible to him and equipping him with the dynamism that comes from the Gospel, if he remains open and obedient to the primacy of the Word who is Christ.

The unity of prophecy and priesthood and its realisation in the Word of the Crucified One is beautifully expressed in a reflection on the theology of ordination by Adrienne von Speyer whose theology of the Cross is so intertwined with that of Balthasar. Von Speyer writes:

The Son's cry is a prophecy, an anticipation, bearing *in advance*, all that will happen to those who are his, who really belong to him, taking seriously the risk of discipleship – all those who were willing to dedicate themselves and now find themselves faced with the void,

10 Hans Urs von Balthasar, *In Gottes Einsatz leben* (Einsiedeln: Johannes Verlag, 1971) ET *Engagement with God* (London: SPCK, 1978), p. 86.

because they chose the void out of love for mankind; because they did not want human security and company but the naked will of God. And this has led them where they did not wish to go.[11]

This evokes clearly the elements of the call of Peter and the dynamics of the Office of pastoral care. For Balthasar the place of Office makes clear what authority really means and what position the teacher and leader must occupy if he is to exercise such authority properly. The priest as Teacher knows, Balthasar states, 'in what currency spiritual power has to be paid for.' Quoting Paul, Balthasar continues:

For this reason I am content with weaknesses, with insults, with hardships, with persecution and fears for Christ's sake, for if I am weak, then I am strong (2 Cor. 12.10). And finally, to make all things quite clear, 'we rejoice when we are weak and you are strong' (2 Cor. 13.9); for this is the meaning of the authority of the ministerial office, which is a spiritual, Christian power only to be exercised for the benefit of others who by it may become strong – which, however, ultimately means for them too that they must become weak, that they must be crucified with Christ, that they must share in bearing the guilt of all.[12]

According to Balthasar, the weight of pastoral Office becomes heavier than any man even in official position can bear. Therefore it is no longer the man who bears the Cross, but the Cross which bears the man. The priest in his public role as Office-holder in the community bears the crisis and the cost of prophecy by his presence and fidelity to the Word made flesh and dwelling among us in the loved but broken community of the Church.

THE PRIEST AS MINISTER OF RECONCILIATION

In Catholic tradition the diocesan priest is intimately identified with the ministry of reconciliation. As Reconciler the priest proclaims in the midst of the Eucharistic Assembly the mercy of God that gathers

11 Adrienne von Speyer, *The Cross: Word and Sacrament* (San Francisco: Ignatius Press, 1981), p. 40.
12 Hans Urs von Balthasar, *Klarstellungen* (Freiburg-im-Breisgau: Verlag Herder KG, 1971), pp. 102–103.

together a people to take away their sins. As Reconciler in the Sacrament of Penance the priest *in persona Christi* speaks the words of absolution that encounter the penitent at the very depth of his being; at the same time, embracing him in the name of the community, the priest stands in relation to the father of the prodigal and proclaims the joy in heaven at the return of the one who was lost. According to Balthasar the priest's authority to forgive sin in the name of Christ and of the Church unfolds from the utmost bounds of Triune love, and therefore touches the very being of the priest himself as he engages in the mysteries of the divine exchange which is always atoning and costly.

The Old Testament antecedents for Atonement are an important clue to depth of engagement with sin that Christian faith considers to be at the heart of its redemptive ministry. The Old Testament liturgies of Atonement hang upon two governing and iconic texts: the sacrifice of Isaac in Genesis 22 and the need for a means of dealing with the sin of the Congregation in worshipping the Golden Calf in Exodus 32–34. In the former, the 'ram (the *agnus dei*), caught by its horns in a thicket' is sacrificed by Abraham 'in the stead of his son', by which is understood that the one becomes the other, particularly since both son and ram are 'God-provided'. In the latter, Moses, after summoning his brethren the Levites to bring the House of Israel back into 'order', must then stand before the Lord and declare: 'This people have committed a great sin; if You will forgive them, please forgive them (they did not know what they were doing). And if not, wipe my name from the Book (of Life) which You have written', that is, take my life in the stead of theirs. It is significant that the Lord accepts the principle of substitutionary atonement here, but the sacrifice to be acceptable is 'the one who has sinned against me', that is Aaron, now become the High Priest of Israel, who gives his life by means of the Atonement animal sacrifice annually as ransom for the people of God in order to reconcile them with their heavenly Father.[13]

Jesus is the Lamb of God who takes away the sins of the world; Balthasar's unique grasp of the theology of substitution and expiation has shown itself to be in response not only to the witness of the New

13 I am here as elsewhere indebted to the Old Testament exegetical insights of Dr Peter Burrows in his unpublished dissertation, 'The Feast of Sukkoth in Rabbinic and Related Literature'. This inclusion of the principle of substitutionary atonement runs contrary to models of atonement that emphasise the positive and transforming dimensions of Jesus' solidarity with sinners. These models, however, while certainly the option for most contemporary theologies of ministry, sacrament and word, are not consistent with Balthasar's highly distinctive theology of the Atonement.

Testament, but also to the tragedies of sin in the structure and fabric of the world. The quality of the loving obedience of the Son of God towards the Father leads the Son to descend into solidarity with the sinful and the lost. As the Lamb of God, he is stripped by the Cross of every power and initiative of his own; he is one purely to be used and it is in exactly this way that he disturbs the absolute loneliness sought for by the sinner. The sinner, therefore, who wants to be damned apart from God, finds God again in the heart of his loneliness. It is here that the full meaning of the *pro nobis* of the event of the Cross is disclosed; Jesus Christ has to be truly human, for only in that way could he take on himself and suffer from within the vicarious experience of the world's sin. But he must also be more than a human being, more than a creature. He must be the unblemished Lamb of God, everywhere to be found in the illusions to a mysterious substitution in the Old Testament and coming to fulfilment in the absolute solidarity of Jesus with his heavenly Father who is now revealed as the Father of all, the lost and the condemned.

The Christian priest cannot remain distant from the mystery of the Atonement that he celebrates. He has to meet many people in his pastoral life and especially in the confessional, for whom God is immensely distant, obscure and 'dead'. In his person, after the manner of Jesus, the priest, the 'lamb' and the reconciliation with the Father, the priest as Reconciler will certainly experience for himself in the darkness of faith the solidarity with those who find faith difficult or who have lost their way. As Confessor he experiences in his own body, so to speak, the struggle with sin and the reaching out for God. As Absolver he is called to experience the compassion of the God who first reaches out towards the sinner.

Living this mystery in the ordinary context of parish and community life often brings the diocesan priest into the hidden depths of the reality of sin and its burden too heavy to bear in the lives of God's faithful people. If the image of the waiting Father is obscured in his own life, then the consciousness of sin and of the need for forgiveness will begin to disappear in the awareness of the community. For Balthasar the bright mirror of love reveals in sharp contours what sin is, but it reveals it now as something that is already in the process of breaking up. The sinner whose sin has been uncovered, Balthasar says, is already as it were in advance wrapped in the protective cloak of his Father. At a time when the Church quite rightly emphasises the communal dimensions of sin as it affects and hurts the whole body of Christ, the more personal dimensions of the healing of the wounds of sin need to be reaffirmed in the pastoral consciousness of the local church and its leaders. What Balthasar offers to the ministerial priesthood in its ministry of reconciliation is a language that is both biblical and existential, which also has the power to speak to and to touch the experiences of abandonment and despair, which in a world of sin cannot be simply avoided by retreating into community and mere activism, even if it is directed to the coming of the Kingdom.

Jesus certainly preached the coming of the Kingdom and in so doing confronted the structures of political oppression and religious hypocrisy. But he also spoke in whispers to sinners and drew quietly and gently with his finger in the sand the words, not of condemnation, but of forgiveness. Echoing this voice that speaks of peace is an intrinsic dimension to the proclamation of the whole Gospel of Christ. Allowing the word of reconciliation to echo from his lips, the priest must first allow it to become flesh in his heart. As a loved sinner, like Peter having turned to the Lord and found the secret of his mercy, the priest learns to give what he has first received.

The recent encouragement of the Holy Father to priests that they themselves should seek the consolation, challenge and strength of the Sacrament of Penance, is a merciful exhortation indeed. Diocesan priests who so often meet the brokenness of sin in the lives of others, need to know where to go with their own burden and to find the Lord as truly their brother and friend. Learning the art of communicating the mercy of God to others is first a matter of learning the depths of God's mercy for oneself. Balthasar gives beautiful expression to this dimension in the life of the priest when he writes:

> His experience with God has taught him what the darkness is like in which one can only find one's way by holding close to the walls, walls which sometimes in the darkness are no longer there, so that one fumbles around and finds no support; such experience is given to the priest in order that in humility he may lend strength to the brother with whom he watches.[14]

THE PRIEST AND HOLINESS

The priest in the minds and hearts of the faithful is identified particularly as a man of intercessory prayer, both in the service of the altar and in the celebration of the divine office. As we have already seen in Balthasar, there is an essential unity between the ecclesial

---

14 Hans Urs von Balthasar, *Klarstellungen*, p. 110.

mission of the priest and a life of interiority. This interiority is understood always as having the contours of the Lord's own inner attitude of obediential love which is the foundation of his being 'for others' and 'for all'. The priest, in his pastoral office, is very much a public figure, a symbol of the institutional presence of the Church in the world, and it is necessary for him to cultivate a deep sense of interiority and identity if he is to fulfil his ecclesial and official mission. For Balthasar this is nothing less than the way of kenosis and of humble presence. In an earlier piety,[15] the priest in his parish was encouraged to take on himself the heart and mind of Jesus, to live a life centred only on him so as to be free in whatever activity or tasks that the apostolate demanded to follow the Master, to be with the Lord. The inner life of the priest took on the form of sacrificial love. His whole life is to become an oblation.

This vision continues to be set before the priesthood as a pastoral inspiration for contemporary ministry by the *Magisterium* of the Church. Priesthood continues to be understood as a spirituality and not merely a task-oriented role or function. Holiness of life, centred on Christ the Good Shepherd remains the norm of priestly existence. In the words of John Paul II:

> God promises the Church not just any sort of shepherds, but shepherds 'after his own heart'. And God's 'heart' has revealed itself to us fully in the heart of Christ the Good Shepherd. Christ's heart continues today to have compassion for the multitudes and to give them the bread of truth, the bread of love, the bread of life (cf. Mk. 6:30ff.), and it pleads to be allowed to beat in other hearts – priests' hearts: 'You give them something to eat' (Mk 6:37). People need to come out of their anonymity and fear. They need to be known and called by name, to walk in safety along the paths of life, to be found again if they have become lost, to be loved, to receive salvation as the supreme gift of God's love. All this is done by Jesus, the Good Shepherd – by himself and by his priests with him.[16]

The interiorisation demanded by this vision of priesthood is rooted in biblical tradition where from the origins of the cult of Israel, holiness was understood to be both the possibility of and the fruit of the engagement of God with His people. Cultic holiness required the

15 Cf. Dom Columba Marmion, OSB, *Christ the Ideal of the Priest* (London: Sands and Co., 1952).
16 *Pastores Dabo Vobis*, p. 82.

interiorisation of a sacrificial offering to God, the sacrifice indeed of a humble and contrite heart. The prophetic call, often to be heard in the priestly circle, constantly reaffirmed the interior conditions for the holiness of worship and the whole life of the people of God. These Old Testament antecedents for priestly holiness cast great light on the interiority of Jesus himself in his priestly role. The liturgy of his own filial love, crying out to the Father in loud tears is certainly a spirituality 'of the heart' and speaks of the most profound depths of interiority in the original ministry and mission of Jesus himself.

This hidden life with the Father comes to full expression in his public ministry of forgiveness and healing, and remains a fundamental characteristic of all ministry in Jesus' name. The diocesan priest called to be near and to live beside God's holy people is invited by that very calling to draw near the Father's heart; in that way the priest lives out the full mission of the Son who is nearest the Father's heart (Jn 1.18). The hidden life of contemplation, prayerful intercession and interior self-giving are therefore understood as not simply the condition for greater pastoral effectiveness or availability although these might well be the secondary fruits of living so deeply in the Lord. In Balthasar's view they are in themselves the most powerful actualisation of pastoral love, for it is through prayer that the priest is drawn into the mystery of Triune love, and it is in loving Christ above all things that he brings forth spiritual fruitfulness in the life of the Church. Balthasar writes about Christian prayer as having no other content than the pure love of God for its own sake:

> ... than pure praise and pure worship of God even beyond every intention of representing the society of the Church or of fulfilling a task within that society.[17]

Balthasar continues to affirm that such depths of contemplative love remain the foundation on which all other Christian activities rest, exposing to view for all to see the foundations particularly of the Eucharist and the ministry of the Church.

Cultivating a spirit of prayer in priestly life is therefore an essential characteristic of authentic spirituality and grounds priestly presence in the very depths of Triune love. Karl Rahner[18] has argued that if priesthood does not have a mystical dimension, then it has nothing at all, a principle found also in Balthasar's reflections on priesthood which

---

17 Hans Urs von Balthasar, *Klarstellungen*, p. 133.
18 Karl Rahner, *Servants of the Lord* (London: Burns and Oates, 1968).

intimately connect the interiority of priesthood with the Evangelical Counsels. Celibacy, obedience and poverty are appropriate to the priest's state of life because they leave him empty and open for God and His purposes. Balthasar situates the appropriateness of the Evangelical Counsels for priestly existence not within a merely juridical concept of order and discipline, but as a radical expression of a life of following. The placing of no conditions which first takes place in the surrender of the heart takes shape in a concrete life form which strives to leave everything and to follow him (Mk 1.17–20; 2.14; Lk 5.11; Mt 19.27). For Balthasar, it is Jesus who brings the fullness of love to perfection on the Cross with a complete exterior and interior emptying of self who is both the model and source of the life of chastity, obedience and poverty. The priest in striving to empty his own self finds in the life of the Evangelical Counsels the road both to union with God in His heart and to loving charity with his brothers and sisters.

The priest then, as Mystic, is an image that corresponds to the radicalism of the Gospel and the highest ideals of pastoral love. Rather than distancing the pastoral priest from the needs and cares of his people, this mysticism leads him to a bond of love that less transcendent models of engagement might not sustain.

INTIMACY AND IDENTITY IN THE LIFE OF THE PRIEST

In recent Church documents the issue of a crisis of identity and of numerical strength in the ministerial priesthood has been explored in order to address what has become in some parts of the Church an urgent problem. The most judicious commentators in the field of the care of clergy who face issues of vocational, emotional or life development crisis, point to a deeply felt sense of lack or loss of identity and self-esteem at the root of this contemporary phenomenon.[19] They believe that a paradigm of discipleship was often embraced that omitted the primacy of the dimensions of intimacy and friendship with the Lord and above all the gift of his unconditional love which the Gospel traditions clearly affirm as characteristic of his relationship with his disciples and friends. Before it is a programme of action or a process

---

19 Adrian Van Kaam, Henri Nouwen and Bernard J. Bush are among many commentators in this field who have made a significant contribution to the integration of spirituality with the behavioural sciences, in positive response to the issues of affectivity, intimacy and development which face clergy today.

leading to personal perfection, discipleship is a call to intimacy and to an identity that will unfold in a life that however costly and Cross-centred, is nevertheless a joyful affirmation of the human possibilities of living in and for Christ.

The personal crisis often emerges in the life of a pastoral priest at mid-life when perhaps the earlier dreams and enthusiasm no longer can sustain the fidelity and pastoral zeal that ministry still asks. He may have discovered the truth about Christian priesthood that it keeps the wounds of the heart open and this discovery may lead him to want to resolve the pain of his existence without necessarily knowing that it is only in a stance of waiting that the purpose of God is revealed. The literature on what has been called the second journey constantly points out both the risk as well as the potential for reaching this point on the journey of life and of faith.

It is here that Balthasar invites the priest in the midst of his apostolic labours and personal struggles to turn to the pathways of Christian spiritual tradition. The great themes of desert, of exile, of learning to sing the Lord's song in a strange land, the experience of Jesus himself at the beginning of his ministry being led by the Spirit into the desert, the language of trial, of drinking the cup that Jesus drinks, all of these run through Balthasar's spiritual theology as a thread that can be also woven into life and its pain and potential.

Balthasar finally offers to the priesthood the image of Mary,[20] who became both the servant and the disciple of the Word to the point of conceiving in her heart and in her womb, the Word made flesh. She beckons the priest in the frailty of his humanity to say with her: 'Yes', to the providence and purposes of God in the mystery of His elective love. Balthasar also emphasises Mary's role in forming, educating, nurturing and loving her son/priest into the fullness of his humanity. Priests are called to have a strong and tender devotion to Mary and to find in her the affirmation of their own personal identity which in Christ comes to fulfilment through the spousal love of the Church to which and for which they are called to give their whole lives.

---

20 A fine presentation of this may be found in John Saward, *The Mysteries of March* (London: Collins, 1990) in a chapter entitled 'Mary, the Mass and the Mysteries of March'.

VII

THE DYNAMIC OF TRADITION

INTRODUCTION

This chapter is an attempt to glimpse something of the unity of Balthasar's thinking in relation to the ministerial priesthood and the question of its interpretation. It is not intended to be a summary, but is rather an effort at detecting the main motifs within the symphonic whole of his theological work.

The approach of Balthasar to the place and paradox of office in the life of the Church is part of a general theological vision which perceives the whole of salvation in the light of the mystery of elective love in which some are called, but only for the sake of all. The divine election of all does not rule out the particularity of chosenness, but rather is grounded in its human and historical, concrete reality. Balthasar establishes the theological coherence of this vision on the presence of its dynamic throughout the whole of Sacred Tradition, from the choice of Israel to the offer of salvation to all in Christ and in the eschatological future of the Church, when God will be all in all.

This sense of Tradition raises the critical issue of the relationship between the Old and New Covenants, which in the context of Christian priesthood is not merely a speculative one. One of the concerns of contemporary spirituality of priesthood is to resolve the question of its compatibility as a new and radical mode of priesthood with the Old Testament antecedents of cultic priesthood and sacrifice. The way in which it moved to resolve this tension has direct consequences on its identity and praxis; fundamentally, an absence of an engagement with the Old Testament form of priesthood and sacrifice leads Christian priesthood to lose its sense of rootedness, not only in the soil of the Sacred, but also of simply human religious aspirations and sentiments.

This problematic has been forcefully raised by Joseph Ratzinger in his *Ministers of Your Joy: Reflections on Priestly Spirituality*, where he writes:

> The reason why this is so significant is that a main reason for the crisis of the image of the priesthood that has its roots in exegesis

and theology was the separation of the Old Testament from the New, with their relationship coming to be seen only in the dialectical tension and opposition of Law and Gospel. Indeed, the unimpeachable refutation of the Catholic idea of priesthood seemed to be the fact that this could be represented as a relapse into Old Testament ways. Christology, it was said, meant the final and definitive transcending of all priesthood, the abolition of the boundaries between sacred and profane, and also the turning away from the entire history of religion in its various forms and their idea of priesthood. Whenever in the Church's image of the priesthood links could be established with the Old Testament or with the heritage of other religions, this counted as a sign that the Church was failing to bring out what was specifically Christian and as an argument against the Church's image of the priest.[1]

Ratzinger argues that such a dichotomy leads to the priesthood being cut off from the entire source of biblical piety and human experience that sacred tradition offers. This banishment to secularity contradicts the essential understanding of the Sacred in Judaic-Christian tradition which Louis Bouyer describes as standing for the sacredness of a God who is not foreign to man, but is his Creator.

> It is revealed in the historical process; historical events take on the precise meaning of signifying God's re-entry into the history of man estranged from Him ... Christian sacredness does not therefore constitute a world beside the world, a life separated from life.[2]

Thus Bouyer has affirmed the integrity and humanism of the Sacred Tradition, a tradition which Balthasar restores to its rightful and central place in the interpretation of ecclesial and ministerial reality.

The purpose of this final chapter is to situate the spirituality of ministerial priesthood within this understanding of the dynamic of Sacred Tradition. In the first place, we shall attempt to affirm the unity and integrity of tradition. Having established its fundamental continuity, we shall move on to explore the contours of the mystery of elective love which Balthasar believes clarifies the identity and

1 Joseph Ratzinger, *Ministers of Your Joy: Reflections on Priestly Ministry* (Slough: St Paul's Publications, 1988), p. 120.
2 Louis Bouyer, 'Note on the Sacred', in *International Theological Commission on Priestly Ministry, 1970* (San Francisco: Ignatius Press, 1989), p. 20.

particularity of priestly ministry in the Church, where the paradox of elective love as the choice of some out of love and for the sake of all continues to unfold. Finally, we shall attempt to uncover from the core of Sacred Tradition its interpretative function which Balthasar holds to be the hermeneutical key to authentically interpreting the present crisis in ecclesial and ministerial identity. He believes the gift of Sacred Tradition to be its grasp of such moments in the self-understanding and development of the Church as primarily an opportunity to enter more deeply into the depth of the Paschal mystery in its full and Catholic wholeness and unity.[3] Such a language for spirituality is certainly one of the Cross; it is also a language of hope for the ministry of the Church in search of its way.

THE PARADOX OF CONTINUITY

The unity and integrity of Sacred Tradition have bearing upon the whole question of not only the future shape of Christian priesthood within the Church, but indeed the continuing validity of the images and language of priesthood itself. The view that the concept of priesthood is ultimately a concession on the part of the Church to a kind of residual paganism that Christianity needs to outgrow, is emerging throughout a wide spectrum of theological analysis of the roots and meaning of Christian ministry.[4]

This view of priesthood as an unnecessary and outmoded model for Christian ministry questions the validity of any cultic or sacral language to describe Christian action in the world. The question of the use of and the justification of priestly language seems, then, to hinge on the broader question of the continuity of tradition and to what extent we can dismiss or ignore these dimensions of Sacred Tradition in our search for authentically interpreting the realities of faith. In the context of ministerial priesthood the question becomes whether we can continue to interpret the radical and new definitive priesthood of Christ in terms of the Old Testament antecedents which have, up until now, had a place in the Catholic theology of priesthood.

Can ministerial priests who participate in the once and forever Priesthood of Christ find any clues to their identity in the roots of Old

---

3 This perception of the unity of theology and of experience is a particular characteristic of Balthasar's Christology; cf. G. Marchesi, *La cristologia di H. Urs von Balthasar* (Roma, 1977).
4 Nicholas Harvey, 'Women's Ordination: A Sideways Look', *The Month*, June (1991), pp. 232–235.

Covenant worship and cultic priesthood? The guiding principle in our finding these clues lies in the theological idiom and interpretation of the author of the Epistle to the Hebrews which may be identified as a fundamental discontinuity that underlies a real continuity.

> Old Testament sayings and events are the primary tools for understanding the mystery of Christ from end to end of the New Testament. There is thus a very real measure of continuity and this also in the matter of the priestly and sacrificial understanding of the mystery of the event of the cross ... But there is a saying of Jesus about the impossibility of putting new wine into old leathers that forever forbids us to forget the even more radical discontinuity between the institutions of the Old Testament and the Gospel event itself.[5]

For the Epistle to the Hebrews, it is the vivid apprehension of the full humanity of Jesus who, in priestly and cultic terms, once and for all puts away sin by the sacrifice of himself. Therefore the priestly language of the New Testament is an intrinsic part of the language of redemption. The notions of sacrifice, priesthood, worship and cult in their Old Testament form are not adequate to interpret the total soteriological event of Christ coming into the world; but they remain one of the most powerful interpretative resources of the Christian tradition and to be part of Christian experience is itself to participate in the experience of redemption normatively expressed in these traditions of Old Testament faith and worship.[6] Without them aspects of redemptive love would be hidden from Christian consciousness. Their value lies in what they continue to give expression to in the word painting of Christian redemptive experience.

The paradox of continuity and discontinuity in the Old and New Covenants need not prevent us from perceiving Sacred Tradition as an unbroken and dynamic 'whole'. To view the inclusion of a priestly cultic language with its antecedents in the Old Covenant as a regression and a manifestation of the incompleteness of the Church's conversion is ultimately to undervalue those very experiences and symbols which gave Jesus his own human and immediate religious consciousness in which came to expression that filial relationship to the Father that became the ground of his understanding of his own life as a sacrifice which would be a ransom for many.

5 Cf. Jerome Smith, OP, *A Priest Forever* (London: Sheed and Ward, 1969).
6 For a classic account of the development of the soteriological images and titles of Jesus, cf. Vincent Taylor, *The Names of Jesus* (London: Macmillan, 1954).

As the International Theological Commission on Priestly Ministry affirms: The diverse soteriological functions of the Old Testament were not simply liquidated by Christ; they were rather taken up and perfected from within by his eminent dignity which made possible an abasement and thereby a ministry without parallel. The radical novelty of a priesthood founded on the divine Sonship appears everywhere, while at the same time the continuity with the traditions of Israel is made manifest.[7]

Christian belief, therefore, that God's revelation of love is given a culminating focus in the person of Jesus does not exclude the other mediations of God's love within history, especially those moments in which the experience of this divine love has become intensified and made transparent. In other words, the priestly work of Christ takes up and recapitulates in its unique structure the religious attitudes, personal and communal, of the faith of Israel and without denying them brings them into a new and ideal fruition. In Balthasar's own words:

Toward this center all the main themes of election in the Old Covenant converge. They point to the mystery: they do not exhaust it. There are, for instance, the themes of the election (of the people) to divine sonship, of the Mediator, of the (High) Priest, of vicarious sacrifice, of the prophet and his destiny, of the Suffering Servant; there are the Jewish themes of the atoning quality of the just man's suffering and death, of the devil's domination of the world, of the resurrection of the dead . . . All these ideas create a vocabulary that circles around the unique reality and helps to express it. Old and New Covenants belong together; this means that later atonement theology will not be able to jettison parts of this vocabulary without suffering harm and impoverishment. (And the old vocabulary can hardly be replaced by a new one.) We need to remember, furthermore, that the old concepts point toward a fulfilled reality that, as such, has transcended the temporal and conditional nature of these motifs (for example, the Old Testament priesthood and sacrificial cult) and attained a sphere of permanent validity and intelligibility.[8]

Christianity, by accepting the sacred status of the Judaic tradition,

---

7 *The International Theological Commission, 1970*, p. 34.
8 Cf. Hans Urs von Balthasar, *Theodramatik, vol. III* (Einsiedeln: Johannes Verlag, 1978), p. 240.

acknowledges that its past, present and future history with God is indeed a disclosure of grace.

In a study of the continuing validity of the Jewish covenant from a Christian perspective, John McDade, SJ, shows that

> At its best, the instinct of Catholic Christianity is to rejoice in the complexity and rich fullness which it sees in God's revelation and, in that spirit, to hold together the constitutive elements of God's revelation and to resist a reduction to a simpler pattern, because in their unity the aspects are willed by God for His purposes.[9]

However varied and distinctive the dimensions of the mystery of divine involvement and however divergent they may appear at particular times, the need to set them in mutual and exclusive opposition is unfounded. Instead of rejecting the Old Covenant tradition of priesthood and cult as diametrically opposed to the New, a more authentic option for theology of priesthood is to enter into dialogue with these traditions from the perception of a participant in its richness and depth as an experience and disclosure of God's self-revelation of love.[10]

In a beautiful passage on the unity of the Old and New Covenant and its Christological significance for the creation of the people of the New Covenant for whose service priesthood exists, Balthasar writes:

> When she received Israel's noblest legacy, the Church obtained not only just vegetative sap from the root, but human sap, the life-blood of Israel, mingled with her high consciousness of mission and the dark depths of suffering that this mission entailed. Ultimately they are two chambers of the one heart that beats which indeed beats on the cross of the world, where the dividing wall was broken down and all hatred was overcome in the flesh of the suffering Christ so that in his person, the two are made one in the single new man who is our peace.[11]

Essentially, therefore, Sacred Tradition in this view cannot be separated nor abstracted from the person and experience of Christ himself. To be aware of the dynamic force which inspires and sustains

9 John McDade, 'The Continuing Reality of the Jewish Covenant', *The Month*, Sept./Oct. (1991), pp. 370–382.
10 Ibid.
11 Hans Urs von Balthasar, *Sponsa Verbi* (Einsiedeln: Johannes Verlag, 1960), p. 176.

Sacred Tradition is truly to be part of the dynamic movement towards Christ's form of love which is hidden and is at the very heart of that tradition. Its characteristics are the call to reciprocal though unequal love that is the essential hallmark of biblical holiness, the mystery of elective love which, before it could be conceived as being for the sake of all and to be everywhere, had to have a beginning; a *locus*; a particularity, which, as we shall see, shaped not only Israel's religious consciousness, but also that of Jesus himself.[12]

THE PARADOX OF PARTICULARITY[13]

In *Engagement with God*, a work in which Balthasar elucidates the mystery of divine involvement and its significance for theology, he carefully traces the contours of grace beginning in the Old Covenant with the call of Abram and coming to its fulfilment in Christ.[14] From its origins in the call of Abram, the absolute and initiating call of God unfolds as a call to intimacy and to reciprocal, though unequal relationship. The human being before the God who chooses becomes a revelation of the dynamic of election that is not governed by any obvious principle, but by a free and mysterious sovereign act of choosing that in time is revealed as love, love that in the Old Testament witness has a distinctive and radical quality.[15]

Balthasar describes this initiating love of God as itself the beginnings of revelation.[16] The primordial origins of both the revelation to and the choice of a people is within the particularity of a personal call: the choice of a people required first the call of Abram, the leading of the people from Egypt through the choosing of Moses, who himself had first to be called by God. As the pattern of their individual calls unfold, it becomes clear that it is not for their sake alone, but for the sake of

---

12 For a consideration of the background to Jesus' religious experience, cf. Louis Bouyer, *The Eternal Son* (Indiana: Our Sunday Visitor, 1978). For an insightful reflection on Israel's religious traditions, cf. H.H. Rowley, *Faith in Israel* (London: SCM Press, 1956).

13 The paradox of particularity is at the heart of Balthasar's spiritual theology of election. Whilst it is certainly rooted in the most profoundly personal engagement with God, it is a dynamic that is ordered primarily to mission.

14 Cf. Hans Urs von Balthasar, *In Gottes Einsatz leben* (Einsiedeln: Johannes Verlag, 1971); ET *Engagement with God*, trans. John Haliburton (London: SPCK, 1975).

15 Ibid., p. 27.

16 Ibid., p. 31.

all the people that God initiates a personal and particular elective relationship.[17]

As Balthasar points out, the call to election, while concerned with the whole people, takes place first and foremost in a personal and intimate call, confronting the one chosen at the very depth of his own being, even as the call itself remains fully representative of all. The free choice and initiative of God constitutes the concrete form under which the divine involvement with the world is revealed: in freely choosing Israel God reveals that His act of choosing is not a reality to be deduced or demanded by any obvious historical or evolutionary principle.[18] The choice of Israel is a manifestation of the mysterious depths of God's will to save. It is not even for Israel's sake; but somehow for the sake of divine love in itself, whose reasons lie hidden under the form of grace. In this way Balthasar can speak of the free choice of Israel as primarily not of power but of love.[19]

According to Balthasar, it is within the elements of the call of Israel and in her symbols of covenant faith, that the full and definitive theology of grace that is established in the New Covenant has its first beginnings. In particular, we glimpse something of the inner necessity and paradox of particularity, a particularity that in embryo seems to be only for and in Israel. But even here there is a hint that somehow the characteristic of divine love has indeed a greater horizon.

The choosing of some for the sake of all which for Balthasar provides the interpretative key to the problematic of particularity in the Judaic-Christian tradition comes into clear focus in the religious consciousness of Israel.[20] This interdependence is grounded in the transcendent yet fully personal involvement and will of God to save.

The paradigm or 'Form' of the call of Moses to lead God's people is instructive here. The transcendent God, ineffable and invisible, intends to deliver His people from their bondage in the house of Pharaoh. To do this, He intends to confront directly; yet by the very reason of His invisible transcendence, He would be unrecognisable to the Egyptian king. To accomplish His task, He chooses a talented and available man, Moses, to act on His behalf. When He shares with Moses at the burning bush His plan to redeem His people, and that Moses is to be His agent in the task, Moses replies with the question: 'Who is this "I" that is going to confront Pharaoh?' 'Surely,' he says, 'you don't mean *my* "I"?'; And the transcendent God replies, 'Not your

17 Ibid., pp. 32–35.
18 Ibid., p. 35.
19 Ibid., p. 36.
20 Ibid., p. 27.

"I"; rather My "I AM" is going to Pharaoh. And I have chosen you to carry My "I AM" to Pharaoh and to make It known and visible to him' (Ex. 3:10ff.).[21]

In this the truly biblical view of the relationship between the one chosen and the call of the whole people to salvation is elucidated, the thought of the one and the many which emerging out of the elective consciousness of Israel develops finally into the New Testament and patristic understanding of the inclusive and representative humanity of Christ, the Mediator of the New Covenant.[22] Here, too, we come to see the coherence of Balthasar's notion of particularity, its consistency with the biblical witness and its possibilities for a theology that seeks to understand the particularity of the Church and her ministry in the light of her meaning as the sign of salvation for all.

James B. Torrance describes the horizons of fulfilment unfolding from the depths of Sacred tradition:

> To this end Israel was called out of Egypt as God's Son, and this thought of the one for the many was written deeply into the liturgical practice and sacrificial life of all Israel and interpreted like the Passover in terms of the memory of their redemption and exodus from Egypt. The first-born son symbolised this vicarious role and in turn the Tribe of Levi was elected as the one tribe to act for the many, for all the Sons of Israel, until in the fullness of time God sent His only Son to be the true Israel, the elect servant, the true priest, the first-born of all creation, in whom and through whom God's purposes for all mankind might be brought to fulfilment.[23]

Again in *Engagement with God* Balthasar identifies this process as the fulfilment of the divine involvement initiated in the election of Israel and reaching its consummation in Jesus of Nazareth in whom 'God's word to us becomes simultaneously man's response to him'.[24] Therefore what is fulfilled in the incarnation is not only the longing in Israel for union with God, but indeed the divine longing for union with

21 Dr Peter Burrows, 'The Feast of Sukkoth'. For Balthasar's spiritual theology of the transcendent in ministry, see above, Chapter IV on the consciousness of Paul, in which the use of the personal pronoun resonates with the call of Moses.
22 The idea of the representative humanity of Christ leads Balthasar to his powerful theological reflection on 'the brother for whom Christ died'; cf. *Herrlichkeit, vol III/2* (Einsiedeln: Johannes Verlag, 1967), pp. 432–470.
23 J.B. Torrance, 'The Vicarious Humanity of Christ,' in Thomas F. Torrance, *The Incarnation* (Edinburgh: The Handsel Press, 1981), p. 137.
24 Hans Urs von Balthasar, *In Gottes Einsatz leben*, p. 36.

humanity, which as the most primal faith of the New Testament is crystallised in Christ's complete transparency to the Father's eternal attitude of self-giving love for the salvation of the world. In the terminology of Karl Barth, Jesus is the eternally elected man.[25] Every gesture of Jesus' life is a definitive and irreversible response to the call and elective love of the Father. His whole life is oriented to that hour in which he will no longer have disposition over himself – a moment identified with his passion, but accepted and unconditionally sealed in the eucharistic giving-over of himself. Such a willingness to give transcends and brings into a new light all the limits of the elective response of Israel. For, as Balthasar so poignantly writes, where man himself fails to give himself fully becomes the place where God, who out of love for the world and in fidelity to the covenant, is seen to give Himself fully.

> The fact that Jesus is the ultimate expression of the divine involvement is evident in a doctrine central to primitive, indeed pre-Pauline Christianity and summed up in the phrase *pro nobis*, 'he who did not spare his own Son but gave him up for us all.' (Romans 8:32) . . . the Son's devotion expressing the Father's condescension which proves His overflowing love for the world.[26]

The singularity of Jesus constantly requires the horizons of Sacred Tradition so that what is seen to bring fulfilment can be understood only together with what it fulfils.

In Balthasar's eyes, the contours of divine election resolve for Christianity the issue and scandal of 'particularity', that God in choosing some appears to be excluding others.[27] This particularity first expressed in the chosenness of Israel comes to its most apparent form in the beloved Son and in the call of the Church which appears to be at one level a rejection of the people first chosen and loved. The call of the Apostles and of those who continue to be entrusted with office might at first hand seem to be elitist or exclusive. For Balthasar this differentiation can only be understood as a form of the essential paradox

---

25 Cf. Karl Barth, *Kirchliche Dogmatik* IV/1.

26 Hans Urs von Balthasar, *In Gottes Einsatz leben*, p. 36.

27 This apparent exclusion of others for the sake of some leads Balthasar in his theology of election to identify with the agony of Paul in Romans as to Israel's fate. It is a crisis that Balthasar perceives to be at the heart of Christian revelation; cf. *Sponsa Verbi*, pp. 166–176. He perceives this principle to be at the core of Christian mystical tradition, an instance of which he finds particularly in the spirituality of Thérèse of Lisieux; cf. *Thérèse of Lisieux: A Story of a Mission* (London: Sheed and Ward, 1956).

of grace which from its very origins in Israel's election bears the mystery of elective love where some are called, but only for the sake of and out of love for all.[28]

Keeping alive the paradox of particularity sustains the reality of divine involvement which, for the sake of all, takes hold of the concrete and personal lives of those whose calling exists only for the sake of others. The kenosis dimension emerges clearly here, especially in the context of the ecclesial mission of the Christian priest who is called only to be a servant of all. That this service has its own distinctive 'Form' is to be understood only in the light of what is at stake: elective love bears within its chosenness the crisis of divine love for all, and the weight of this involvement requires that election never forgets its essence as responsibility and not status, as having no other purpose than to exist, not for itself, but only for the sake of others.[29]

The dynamic that drives the Church and her ministry towards this place of service and love where it no longer exists as an end in itself but as salvation for the whole world, is the dynamic that brought Israel first into being, a dynamic that shaped the ministry and mission of Jesus himself – a sacred tradition that continues to unfold in the lives of those chosen and called.[30]

INTERPRETATION AND TRADITION

One of the significant purposes of Sacred Tradition in Christian theology is, for Balthasar, that it summons the Church to discover in the Christ-Form her own underlying reality. According to Balthasar, 'testing the Spirit', discerning the will of God for both personal and ecclesial existence takes place within the orbit of Trinitarian self-giving love. Sacred Tradition takes hold of Ecclesiology and plunges it into the Trinitarian mystery of love. The 'rule' of that love, the Holy Spirit, guided the human heart and destiny of Jesus and continues to lead the Church into the Truth.[31] Whilst this need not be seen in opposition to secular developments or the 'signs of the times', the criterion of discernment is certainly beyond the grasp or attainment of merely human speculation and insights.

In Balthasar's view, the flow of Sacred Tradition and its direction

28 Hans Urs von Balthasar, *In Gottes Einsatz leben*, p. 39.
29 Ibid., p. 49.
30 Ibid., p. 81.
31 Cf. Hans Urs von Balthasar, *Pneuma und Institution* (Einsiedeln: Johannes Verlag, 1974), pp. 55–58.

is often hidden from view. Only the inner eye of faith can hope to see dimly and must wait to be opened, and thus allowed to glimpse the ultimate, final, yet originating Form of what is holy and true, ultimately the will and prayer of Christ for his Church. Any sense of simply reading the 'signs of the times' is thought by Balthasar to be too blunt an instrument.[32] Any value it has can only emerge through the endurance of the dark night of faith, by entering more deeply into the Paschal mystery and finding at the heart of its existence the signs of crucified love which is the hope of the world.

When Christian reflection asks in faith where this insight is being made accessible, Balthasar turns our attention to the openings given to us in Sacred Tradition itself, a tradition which ultimately seeks to ground faith in the Triune God and His involvement with the world in the context of the person and humanity of Jesus.[33] Engagement with the dynamic of Sacred Tradition leads ultimately to a participation in the vocation and destiny of Jesus himself and roots ecclesial and personal experience in Jesus' own human experience of God.[34]

At the core of this tradition, Balthasar perceives the mysteries of the Lord's passion, death, descent into hell, resurrection and glorification; the Church not only lives out these experiences, but they mirror to her the mysteries of love of which she is both the promise and the fruit.[35] Every characteristic of the Lord's mission is meant for the Church to bring out in her the contours of his mission, and thus to fulfil the Father's will. For Balthasar, the Lord has taken the Church with him into the Cross, and therefore into his glory.[36]

It is therefore essential for the Church to be able to interpret her experience in history and in the world in the light of the Christ-Form, within the horizons of Sacred Tradition. Balthasar identifies the present

---

32 Cf. A study of Balthasar's perception of the role of tradition in the interpretation of the signs of the times is to be found in David Brown, *Continental Philosophy and Modern Theology* (Oxford: Blackwell, 1989).

33 Cf. Hans Urs von Balthasar, *Kennt uns Jesus – Kennen wir ihn?* Freiburg-im-Breisgau: Verlag Herder, 1980); ET *Does Jesus Know Us? Do We Know Him?* trans. Graham Harrison (San Francisco: Ignatius Press, 1983), pp. 61–94.

34 Ibid.

35 Balthasar sees himself as indebted to Adrienne von Speyer in his theological insights into the mystery of the Cross and its significance for the shape of the Church's presence and mission in the world. His appropriation of her mystical insights into Ecclesiology is well documented. Cf. Johan Roten, 'Marian Anthropological Dimensions in the Common Mission of Adrienne von Speyer and Hans Urs von Balthasar', *Communio*, XVI (1989), pp. 420–445. See also Adrienne von Speyer, *The Cross, Word and Sacrament* (San Francisco: Ignatius Press, 1981), pp. 37–49, where Adrienne reflects on the contours of priesthood in the light of the contours of the Cross.

36 Ibid., p. 39.

moment in the Church's development and history as one of obvious
vulnerability and believes that only in the depths of the tradition will
she find the interpretative key to this, her time of institutional frailty
and fragmentation. According to Balthasar, it is not only a matter of
perceiving the 'whole' of the Christ event in its fragments and
brokenness – rather he speaks paradoxically of 'the whole' *as* fragment.[37]
In this way he holds that a church brought to a place of frailty, crisis
and humiliation might in fact correspond more fully to the original
form of the Church, powerless and born only out of crucified love –
the Church of the Gospel, the community of faith gathered around
the Cross in order that God might in time gather the whole world to
Himself in it and in love. A Church transparent to these radical
traditions is, in Balthasar's perspective, a Church at the heart of the
world; solidarity with the world takes on, in the light of these
traditions, a depth and an urgency that challenges Christian ministry
and praxis to turn again to the central mysteries of the Cross and
Resurrection, and find there the motivation to become more fully a
ministry of the Gospel of Christ and him crucified.[38]

The authors of *Spiritual Renewal of the American Priesthood* believe
that there is a need today for priests to recapture a sense of how the
mysteries of Christ are being re-enacted in the mysteries of their own
lives:

Pope Paul VI reminded us that only faith can tell us who we are
and what we should be . . . 'Look to Jesus the Pioneer and Perfection
of our faith . . .'. The Jesus in question is the living Christ, alive
among us and in us, who bears within himself his historical earthly
existence with the marks of the mysteries of his death upon him.
The authentic disciple attempts to understand how the mysteries of
Jesus are being re-enacted in the mysteries of his own life.[39]

This perspective does not in any sense resolve the acute pastoral

37 Cf. Hans Urs von Balthasar, *Das Ganze im Fragment* (Einsiedeln: Johannes Verlag,
1963); ET *Man in History*, trans. William Glen Doepel (London: Sheed and Ward,
1972).
38 It is at this level of the interpretation of the role of the Cross in Christian
redemption that Balthasar understands himself to differ from Rahner, cf. Hans Urs
von Balthasar, *Theodramatik, vol. III*, pp. 273–284. For a consideration of both their
similarities and their contrasts, cf. Rowan Williams, 'Balthasar and Rahner', in *The
Analogy of Faith*, ed. John Riches (Edinburgh: T. & T. Clark, 1986), pp. 11–35.
39 Cf. *Spiritual Renewal of the American Priesthood*, ed. Ernest Larkin (Washington,
D.C.: U.S. Bishops Conference, 1973), pp. 39–40.

problems of the Church in our day of post-Christian apathy. But it does provide an horizon that makes transparent the essential mystery of Christian and ecclesial reality – Jesus dying as brother of the condemned and the lost, Jesus crucified outside of the holy place – his preferential love for sinners and for the poor who are now considered blessed, taking shape in the community of the Church and in the ministry of her servant priesthood.

It is one of the great insights of liberation theology that the praxis of Christian ministry should begin from around the Cross; speaking of the European Church in relation to its own alienated people, Sobrino suggests that it should learn from a theology of the Paschal mystery that there are no facile recipes or equations for the praxis of the Gospel and the building up of the community of the Church. He proposes that the tired European Church make an act of humility and give up trying to control and programme for pre-conceived results . . . to accept a certain silence of God in our societies and not to force God's word where it cannot be heard.[40]

Balthasar seems to speak about the same reality when he asks the Church to understand that the silence and emptiness of the Holy Saturday experience is not merely a memory of a chronologically distant past, but a necessary moment in the unfolding of the Paschal mystery in her life.[41] He shows how Christian spirituality has constantly contemplated this path between Cross and resurrection, and has come to grasp the essential logic and holiness of the silence and the apparent absence of God, the experience of abandonment and the diminishment in spiritual experience in which only a dull emptiness accompanies the purely human talking and thinking about God.[42] In *Man and History* Balthasar elucidates the meaning of the Holy Saturday experience of Jesus for ecclesial reality; for him it is an intrinsic dimension of the theology of the Cross and is a permanent expression, therefore, of the inwardness of ecclesial life.[43] An ecclesial spirituality at a time of crisis when strategies and words seem to be no longer enough to sustain Christian hope has here within the most profound depths of Christological tradition an image that carries the Church through the dark night of faith and helps her to live creatively through the inevitable temptations to escape its terror and its hopelessness.[44]

40 Jon Sobrino, *Spirituality of Liberation* (New York: Orbis, 1988).
41 Hans Urs von Balthasar, *In Gottes Einsatz leben*, p. 94.
42 Ibid., p. 96.
43 Hans Urs von Balthasar, *Das Ganze im Fragment* (Einsiedeln: Benziger Verlag, 1963) ET *Man in History* (London: Sheed and Ward, 1968).
44 Ibid., pp. 77–78.

Jesus' own unique experience of the dark night of the Cross and the silence of Holy Saturday becomes, in Balthasar's synthesis, the paradigm which authentically interprets the participation of the Church in that self-same experience.[45] He describes the process of the transformation of the tragedy of human existence as an experience that descends into the depths of that which is lost and hopeless, opening up a way for man through the very powers that would otherwise destroy him. He writes:

> The word descends vertically from the highest height, deeper than any mere human word can descend, into the last futility of empty time and hopeless death. This word does not prophetically transfigure death, playing around it: He bores right through it to the bottom, to the chaotic formlessness of the death cry (Matt. 27:50), and to the wordless silence of death on Holy Saturday. Hence he has death in his grip; he dominates it, limits it and takes from it its sting.[46]

Thus Balthasar affirms that Christ has all that is passing and fragile in his hands, not through a poetic or legislative transcendence of time, but by entering into its inner structure of limitation and death. He meditates on the cry of Jesus on the Cross, not as a denial of his presence and teaching to the disciples and to the people, but the fulfilment of all that the cry now articulates.

> A cry of redemption . . . as Omega this cry becomes Alpha, the cry of birth with which the new man breaks through to the light of the world.[47]

Therefore, according to this vision, the Church need not be afraid to die, to share in the passion and death of Jesus. This is not, however, to be understood as simply some cult of failure that in certain literary genres encourages a kind of existential sadness and discouragement in regard to the life of being a Christian, or indeed a priest.[48] It is also far removed from the anxieties of a 'death of God' theology which denies the triumph of love and the promise of resurrection which an authentic theology of the Cross seeks always to promote. It is rather a profound theological interpretation of the fragmentation that touches the very heart of the Church even as it touches the heart of the history

45 Ibid., p. 282.
46 Ibid., p. 283.
47 Ibid.
48 This literary genre is exemplified in the figure of the broken priest in Graham Greene's novel, *The Power and the Glory*.

of the Son of God himself. Balthasar is a theologian who has particularly confronted the dimension of tragedy in both human and salvation history. His emphasis on the place of suffering and death in the Christian life is above all to be seen on his part as a necessary piece of theological logic in the vision of resurrected love which for him both fulfils and discloses the love at the heart of the Theodrama.

As an interpretation of contemporary experience, Balthasar's dramatic and imaginative categories of theological and spiritual exploration may seem to some as too close to religious embroidery that may not correspond to the concrete realities of ecclesial, social and personal living that perhaps a more critical and empirical language might do justice to. The assessment of theologian John Riches, however, points to the power of Balthasar's reflective theology as one that draws us into the Paschal mystery and enables us to see the glory of the Lord which, in Christian terms, illumines the darkness of our world, with all it hopes and fears.

And it is this vision that enables one in turn to see the world, with all its *grandeurs et misères*, as never without grace, always in need of reconciliation and transformation.[49]

The task of perceiving not only the brokenness of the world, but also the brokenness of the Church sent to the world in love, through the prism of this foundational vision of Christian optimism, is one that constantly requires theology keep clear of superficial and facile hermeneutics. The hermeneutic that Balthasar perceives to be at the heart of the Christian tradition interprets the present moment of crisis in the Church as an opportunity to enter more deeply into the Passion of God. Far from conceiving this as a merely pious sentiment, Balthasar understands this process as one of entering into the Passion at the heart of the Triune God for the world. Thus Sacred Tradition roots the ministry of the Church in the most profound depths of the experience of God and of the realities of the real and broken world. The function, therefore, of tradition is to root Christian ministry in reality: it is essentially liberating and open to the world.[50]

49 John Riches, 'Hans Urs von Balthasar', in *The Modern Theologians*, ed. David F. Ford (Oxford: Blackwell, 1989) p. 253.
50 For other writers who grasp the profound significance of Trinitarian theology for the praxis of the Gospel in the world, cf. John O'Donnell, SJ, *The Mystery of the Triune God* (London: Heythrop, 1988); Eberhard Jüngel, *God as the Mystery of the World* (Edinburgh: T. & T. Clark, 1977), and *The Doctrine of the Trinity* (Edinburgh: Scottish Academic Press, 1976).

A LIBERATING TRADITION

Being a man for others does not therefore, in Balthasar's view, make the priest less a man of and for the Church. It is in understanding his ecclesial function correctly, and in the light of the solidarity of the Crucified One, that the priest discovers and affirms his deepest self as union in Christ and with others. His liturgical office, particularly the celebration of the Eucharist, shapes his life within the liturgy of the human heart of Jesus. Congar, writing on the mystery of the Incarnation, speaks of God the Father who gives to the Son the gift of a human heart.[51] In the light of this new humanity in Christ which Schillebeeckx rightly identifies with the coming of the Kingdom into the world, there is also the need to reaffirm the efficacy of the continuing presence of Jesus at the heart of the institutional Church, which itself witnesses to the promise of a new *humanum*, by her presence and ministry in the world. Therefore, to be a minister of the Gospel of Christ and to be a prophet of the new creation, to be an *alter Christus*, a man of the Church, and a man of prayer, to be centred on the altar and to stand under the Cross, is, for the Christian priest, to be committed to the coming of the new *humanum* and to be secularly involved.[52] The priest by his ministry, therefore, is called to refashion the world in Christ.

This synthesis is theoretically viable and possible in praxis only on the grounds of the integrating function of the tradition that has been already identified above. Whilst taking the point made by O'Meara that we need historical liberation in our theology because Christian ministry has been particularly receptive to what we might call a process of eternalisation, it is important to maintain with Balthasar that it is precisely in Sacred Tradition that the liberating and rich origins of ministry in Christ's name remain accessible to the faithful Church. Like O'Meara, Küng and others, Balthasar believes that the death of external structures can be an intrinsic part of the Paschal mystery.[53] What he distinguishes, however, is the eternalisation of cultural forms of ministry arising out of particular historical and social situations

---

51 Cf. Yves Congar, *I Believe in the Holy Spirit, Vol II: The Lord and Giver of Life*, (London: Geoffrey Chapman, 1983), p. 213; In this volume Congar also explores the Holy Spirit as the principle of catholicity in the Church and identifies this principle as one of both the holiness and the freedom of the Church's life and mission.

52 For a comprehensive treatment of the themes of Trinity, Incarnation, transformation and mission in the life of the ministerial priest, cf. Philip Rosato, 'The Spirituality of the Diocesan Priest', *The Way Supplement*, 39 (1980), pp. 91–95.

53 Hans Urs von Balthasar, *In Gottes Einsatz leben*.

which, indeed, may require the priesthood to free itself from its restraints. There is in Balthasar's view a right and proper dimension of eternalisation in Christian interpretation which seeks to sustain the foundational paradigms of mission and ministry. These are beyond cultural and historic mutability. They directly refer to the contours of the continuing presence of Christ and work of the Holy Spirit which are a constant and distinctive determinant in the process of Christian interpretation.

However, there remains the tension of living out of the institutional and charismatic dimensions of the life of the Church. Balthasar identifies these twin elements of ecclesial interpretation as at one and the same time 'determining-institutionalising' and 'liberating-universalising', revealing the presence in the Church of the Holy Spirit, who, in Balthasar's words, is 'the determining form of freedom'. The significance of this vision is one that allows the Church to live creatively towards its future in such a way that the Christian community does not live in slavish imitation of Christ or in a petrified repetition of the past. At the same time, because the Spirit in the community is always bound to Christ, his presence and power always has Christological Form.[54]

Therefore, Balthasar's insistence on the priority of the Christ-Form for the interpretation of the ministerial priesthood and its future development and shape is not a restrictive one and certainly cannot be identified as dismissive of the freedom of the Spirit. Rather, He is more appropriately to be understood in the light of the movement of mission within the life of the Trinity in which the Father does not only send the Son, but the Holy Spirit, the mutual love of Father and Son: the sending of Christ cannot be separated from the action of the Spirit, for it is in the Spirit that the Son of God enters history and becomes man. This mutuality is brought to expression in the life of the Church and sustains the institutional and pneumatological dimensions of its existence in unity and interdependence.[55]

54 Yves Congar, *I Believe in the Holy Spirit, Vol. II*, pp. 24–33.
55 According to Gisbert Greshake, this provides the ministry of the Church with both its objective form and its interiority and freedom – it is what gives tradition its root in Christ and possibilities and future in the gift and promise of the Spirit. Consequently, the people of God is, as it were, shaped by the objective form of Christ and the interior life of the Spirit, by the 'visible organised form' and the 'power of the Spirit'. The outward, objective Christological form communicates and supports the presence of the Spirit, and the Spirit labours to imprint on all the living the form of Christ. Form seeks to become life, life seeks to find form. The two aspects cannot be separated. They are no more inconsistent with each other than the Father, Son and Holy Spirit.' *The Meaning of Christian Priesthood*, (Dublin: Four Courts Press, 1988), p. 86.

LIVING OUT OF TRADITION

The Church has always taught that the Lord, not despite but because of his glorification, is more closely identified with us now than he was in the days of his flesh. The God of the Catholic Christian tradition is a God who became man and suffered, and who now does not stand on his dignity, but bears our burdens with us. And so a spiritual and pastoral 'living-out' of this tradition in no way distances the Church from the world, but allows for an involvement and interaction, which a functional approach cannot offer. In the words of Balthasar:

> The Christian involvement has its origins in God's involvement for the sake of the world. It is grounded in it, captivated by it, shaped and directed by it. He turns therefore with God to the world.[56]

In this way Balthasar is taking up the theme of St Paul who in his writings places ministry in the context of the divine initiative.

> All this is from God, Who through Christ reconciled us to Himself and gave us the ministry of reconciliation. That is, God was, in Christ, reconciling the world to Himself (2 Cor. 5:18).

As Archbishop Michael Ramsey of the Anglican Communion says in his great book, *The Christian Priest Today*[57], 'We are called near to Jesus, and with Jesus, and in Jesus to be with God, with the people on our heart'. Speaking of pastoral love for the world, Ramsey takes the vocation of pastoral priesthood not to its task and goal-oriented terms of reference, but to its roots:

> Your prayer, then, will be a rhythmic movement of all your powers, moving into the divine presence in contemplation and moving into the needs of the people in intercession. In contemplation you will reach into the peace and stillness of God's eternity, in intercession you will reach into the rough and tumble of the world of time and change.[58]

For the Church to go to the world outside itself, there must be something inside it to be externalised. This internal aspect is not itself,

---

56 Hans Urs von Balthasar, *In Gottes Einsatz leben*, p. 67.
57 Michael Ramsey, *The Christian Priest Today* (London: SPCK, 1972).
58 Ibid., p. 14.

but Christ the Head and Heart of the Church. He is present in the inner life of the Church as the *one* who is given by the Father to the world that is so loved (Jn 3:16). To turn with Him towards the world in this love is the ministry of the Church *par excellence*; to have turned to him in love and received him in love in the first place is to make such ministry possible.

The starting point for an authentic Ecclesiology, and therefore an authentic spirituality of the Church, cannot be other than what is given to the Church as pattern of her life and service. This means that the spirituality of the Church cannot be worldly in the sense of power to assert herself with new and promising methods and programmes of political and sociological change. When we pray or plan for the Church, we are called to ask ourselves if our prayer fits in with that of Christ for the Church and begins from there. This has serious implications for the spirituality of the ministerial priesthood, particularly in our time, when the Church calls us to see the mission and function of the priesthood in the context of Ecclesiology: in doing this the Church understands that at the heart of Ecclesiology is Christology, and assumes that in view of the ministry as Church-centred, we see it for that very reason as Christ-centred.

> Faith teaches that Church, whose mystery is being set forth by this sacred synod, is holy in a way which can never fail . . . for Christ . . . who with the Father and the Spirit is praised as being 'alone holy', loved the Church as his bride . . . and body. Therefore, everyone belonging to the hierarchy or being cared for by it is called to holiness.[59]

---

59 This is in a special way the doctrine of the Second Vatican Council contained especially in *Lumen Gentium, Presbyterorum Ordinis* and *Ad Gentem*; also in the Encyclical of Paul VI, *Sacerdotalis Caelibatus* and the Document, 'De Sacerdotio Ministeriali' of the 1971 Synod of Bishops.

CONCLUSION

The whole of Balthasar's theological reflection is directed towards elucidating the Form of Christ at every level and focal point of Christian
and ecclesial living. This Christological concern permeates particularly
his thinking about the ministerial priesthood. Especially in the light
of the recent crisis within the presbyterate, both at a theological and
practical level, Balthasar insists that the debate about and the resolution
of the problem can never be simply a matter of recasting structures
nor an openness to only the urgency of the demands of pastoral ministry.
However significant and legitimate contemporary answers and developments in ministry might be, Balthasar holds out for a constant 'baptism'
of ministerial structure and function into the depths of the essential
Trinitarian and Christological structures of ecclesial reality. The 'Form
of Christ' becomes the foundational hermeneutical principle that guides
the priesthood into the complexities of its future and the relentless
demands of its mission.

This might seem at first sight to be an inhibition on what Balthasar
can think and say about the priesthood in contrast, perhaps, to a
theological starting point that begins with a more pragmatic and
concrete approach to priestly ministry. At one level Balthasar might
seem to be approaching the question from 'above' rather than from
'below', and in so doing he might be at one step removed from the
realities of pastoral life and work that constitute the very heart of the
spirituality of the pastors of the Church. Recent accounts of his work
have certainly been critical of his tendency to understate the existential
and subjective contexts for fruitful theological reflection.[1] Because there
is a tendency in his writing towards being a-historical and without a
prophetic or critical grasp of the socio-political realities of our time,
he may appear to be at a distance from the issues which ministry in
practice cannot evade. Because Balthasar is so clearly intent on interpreting experience in the light of the most profound doctrines of the
Christian faith, it is suggested that he has not sufficiently developed
an understanding of the transformative function of doctrine and robs
it, therefore, of its empowerment to confront the world with the presence of the Kingdom.

1 Cf. Gerard O'Hanlon, SJ, and his assessment of contemporary critiques of von
Balthasar in 'Theological Dramatics', in Bede McGregor, OP, *The Beauty of Christ: An
Introduction to the Theology of Hans Urs von Balthasar* (Edinburgh: T. & T. Clark, 1994),
pp. 92–111.

These judgements, however, need to be qualified by the insights of other theologians who find in Balthasar's theology a unique openness to the world, especially in its most tragic, personal and historical dimensions.[2] While it is not one of Balthasar's strengths to provide the practical elements of the praxis of the Gospel, his more panoramic view of Christian existence gives more of a vision and horizon for the theological reflection that grounds Christian action and service in the radicalism of the Gospel. Furthermore, he opens up the categories of theology to engage fully in and with the world through his consistent interpretation of the Christian mystery of God and His involvement with the world in a Trinitarian and Christological language that holds together both transcendence and immanence, mystery and vulnerability as the essential qualities of Christian presence in and for the world.

How precisely this involvement and presence might take place and shape the structures of ministerial priesthood is a development that goes beyond Balthasar's own agenda. However, the radicalism that it would bring to the life and ministry of priests in terms of servant identity, self-emptying love and spousal commitment to the Church in no sense would contradict Balthasar's original thinking. Rather, the marks of powerlessness and kenosis that would characterise the style of presbyteral spirituality would be wholly consistent with Balthasar's central Christological notions of solidarity and kenosis which mirror to the world the very nature of God. It is this grasp of what Christian openness to the world truly entails that gives to Balthasar's Christological interpretation of the ministerial priesthood its power and its effectiveness. If the ministerial priesthood is at a crossroads in self-understanding concerning its identity and mission, then it is in need, not only of pragmatic models of its function but of horizons and visions of its meaning and its truth.

We have seen how Balthasar's own experience as a ministerial priest may have influenced his particular emphases on certain styles and characteristics of priestly existence. This is fundamentally speculative, but at the same time is sufficiently grounded in the facts of his life both as a person and as a priest, to merit exploration. It may indeed provide a key to at least one door into the antechamber of his mind-set on the priesthood which is a dimension of his thought which often remains problematic for his readers. It is mainly concerned with his tendency to identify the ministerial priesthood 'connaturally' with the

2 Cf. David L. Schindler, ed., *Hans Urs von Balthasar: His Life and Work* (San Francisco: Ignatius Press, 1991). Also John O'Donnell, *Hans Urs von Balthasar* (London, Geoffrey Chapman, 1991).

life of the Evangelical Counsels. This is to place more emphasis than the *magisterium* actually does when it speaks of a connection that is appropriate rather than any sense of an intrinsic bond. Balthasar goes beyond this language towards a more absolute and objective identification, almost placing the state of life of the ministerial priest within the same context of Evangelical living as those in religious life. While we have seen that, on a semantic level, he holds back from explicitly saying this, his intuitive sense seems to blur the distinctions that remain both canonically and existentially clear in Catholic tradition. Balthasar's own experience of being both a religious and a secular priest clearly accounts for his existential sense of integration in this area of identity, which for others can be more problematic. Balthasar considered his whole theological enterprise as a secondary output unfolding from his mission of working for the renewal of the Church with the formation of new communities that united radical Christian living according to the Evangelical Counsels with existence in the midst of the world.

Therefore, it is essential to distinguish in his theological and spiritual reflections on the priesthood what may arise from his own personal sense of his mission and the inevitable sensibilities that this perhaps brought to his theological judgement. It is clear that the circumstances of pastoral life and work that would characterise the ministry of a majority of priests would not have entered into Balthasar's epistemological underpinnings. What he cherished about the priesthood was naturally learnt through his own appropriation of priestly ministry, and this has valuable insights to bear. What cannot be introduced, because it was never learnt, were other dimensions of priestly asceticism and availability.

In a Catholic tradition that continues to sustain a plurality of priestly lifestyles and ministries, which themselves have emerged through a complex and often unclear line of development, Balthasar offers a rich and challenging spirituality that is rooted in a profound and radical sense of discipleship and personal consecration to Christ and a total gift of self to His Church. At the same time he offers a coherent spiritual theology of office that affirms the ontology of the priesthood as well as the fullest possible personal response in the life of the priest himself. Balthasar, because he understands the priesthood as a gift of Christ Himself to the baptised, considers the priesthood to be called to its own distinctive holiness, not as sacred status but as sacred service. His enduring Gospel image at the heart of his Ecclesiology of the constellation around Jesus forming the original Church, the Church of Mary and John gathered around the Cross in powerlessness and love, becomes the place where office must continually find its origins, its bearings and its direction.

That Balthasar's Ecclesiology is so highly symbolic and rests on the polarity of the masculine-feminine principle may appear to be one-sided, and it may be open to the criticism that it has to do with the lack of critical reflection on Balthasar's own part on his own anthropological and ecclesial presuppositions. The recognition that Balthasar's chosen images cannot be applied univocally and with complete adequacy should not however prevent us from seeing that his ecclesial method approaches the mystery of the Church and her ministry that on the conceptual map of contemporary theology needs locating and affirming. In particular, his strikingly comprehensive Marian interpretation of the nature of the Church roots a theology of Institution and Office in the context of its own relativity to the absolute mystery of Christ and his love for the Church, his Body and his Bride. Balthasar himself believed that this interpretative function of the Marian and nuptial dimensions of Ecclesiology saves the Church and her ministry from the temptation to become merely a religious bureaucracy and an organisational tool for the implementation of the programme of the Kingdom. The significance of this model of the Church and its powerful symbolism for the ministerial priesthood cannot be underestimated at a time when the emphasis in ministry tends towards the appropriation of functions and professional skills which in themselves, however valuable, cannot substitute for the miracle of grace which is the mystery of the Church and the priesthood which exists to serve and protect that nuptial mystery.

The need for a more pneumatological theology of the Church and of the priesthood is clearly evident in contemporary Catholic theology and its restoration at the heart of ecclesial interpretation is unquestionably valid. Balthasar's explicitly Christocentric methodology might seem at first glance to neglect the dimensions of the activity and work of the Holy Spirit at the cost of a more static and controlled vision of what the ministerial priesthood does and must entail. If the Spirit's mission is to be ever-creative and if this places the life of the Church continually towards the future, the question may be asked of a more Christ-centred paradigm, whether it inhibits this creativity and openness towards an uncharted future. There is certainly a creative tension surrounding this issue in Catholic theology today and it challenges one of the presuppositions of this thesis that it is only in the mystery of Christ that the priesthood finds its truth. What we need to affirm is Balthasar's understanding of the Holy Spirit as being the norm of everything institutional in the Church. The Spirit is always the Spirit of the Father and the Son, and is therefore the 'rule' of the Son's life and mission from the Father. It is the Spirit who guides Jesus towards his self-giving ministry and who is the source of the boundlessness of the love which is at the heart his kenosis and his Cross. Hence the Christological and pneumatological form an intrinsic unity and are, in Balthasar's view, what both determine and liberate the Church to be most fully herself. Living with the creative tension of this paradox is the way for priesthood to come to its own freedom and truth.

Finally there is the whole area of reflection on priestly spirituality that in recent times has provided both the stimulus and the resources for ministerial development and growth, both in the skills of ministry and in the area of personal and spiritual maturation. The new appreciation of the liturgical and presidential functions of priesthood, the renewed theology of priest as a man of the sacraments, the whole area of mutuality between the ordained ministry and the priesthood of all believers and new patterns of collaborative ministry, all these developments have brought a new vigour to the Christian community and a continuing challenge to the presbyterate.[3] Balthasar, who does not explicitly treat these themes in his theology of ministry, offers a spirituality of institution that integrates function with interiority and which makes of all the elements of ministerial practice the constituents of what he calls 'a service in the Church which is the crystallisation of the love of Christ himself'.

Likewise in the development of holistic spirituality, which has embraced the most creative and judicious insights of the behavioural sciences, the priesthood needs a spiritual and theological context in which to integrate and from which it must constantly draw to renew itself. Balthasar certainly stands in the tradition of a Christian humanism which affirms the value and the essential holiness of the human; however, with this tradition, he would affirm too the costliness of becoming human and holy. It is here that his profound grasp of the experience of God, of human life and of relationships with others, in which he understands everything to be grace, can help priests to understand themselves as persons and personalities, called to full maturity in Christ.

Recognising the limits of Balthasar's method, we come also to perceive where its essential gift lies. For Balthasar the Form of Christ

3 For a clear and penetrating analysis of the post-Conciliar developments of the theology of the ministerial priesthood, especially in the light of the teaching of the recently published Catechism of the Catholic Church, cf., P. Rosato, 'The Sacrament of Orders' in M. Walsh, *Commentary on the Catechism of the Catholic Church* (London: Geoffrey Chapman, 1994), pp. 303–317.

expands and gives to the Church all her possibilities for mission and for ministry. Uncovering the Christ-Form for the life of ministerial priesthood is therefore also an uncovering of its possibilities and the foundations for its dreams.

BIBLIOGRAPHY

SELECTED WORKS OF BALTHASAR

BOOKS (IN ORDER OF PUBLICATION)

Therese von Lisieux, Cologne: Olten, 1950; trans. as *Thérèse of Lisieux: A Story of a Mission*, London: Sheed and Ward, 1956.

Das Betrachtende Gebet, Einsiedeln: Johannes Verlag, 1957; trans. as *Prayer*, A.V. Littledale, London: Geoffrey Chapman, 1961.

Sponsa Verbi, Skizzen zur Theologie, I, Einsiedeln: Johannes Verlag, 1960; trans. as *Church and World*, A.V. Littledale. New York: Herder and Herder, 1967.

Herrlichkeit, Eine theologische Aesthetik, I: Schau der Gestalt, Einsiedeln: Johannes Verlag, 1961; trans. as *The Glory of the Lord, I: Seeing the Form*, Erasmo Leiva-Merikakis, Edinburgh: T. and T. Clark, 1982.

Herrlichkeit. Eine Theologische Aesthetik, II: Facher der Stile, 1: Klerikale Stile, Einsiedeln: Johannes Verlag, 1962; trans. as *The Glory of the Lord, Vol. II: Studies in Theological Style: Clerical Styles*, Andrew Louth, Edinburgh: T. and T. Clark, 1984.

Das Ganze im Fragment, Einsiedeln: Benziger Verlag, 1963; trans. as *Man in History*, William Glen-Doepel, London: Sheed and Ward, 1968.

Glaubhaft is nur Liebe, Einsiedeln: Johannes Verlag, 1963; trans. as *Love Alone: The Way of Revelation*, Alexander Dru, New York: Herder and Herder, 1969.

Wer is ein Christ, Einsiedeln: Johannes Verlag, 1965.

Herrlichkeit. Eine theologische Aesthetik, III/2, I. Teil: Alter bund, Einsiedeln: Johannes Verlag, 1967.

Spiritus Creator. Skizzen zur Theologie, III, Einsiedeln: Johannes Verlag, 1967.

Erster Blick auf Adrienne von Speyer, Einsiedeln: Johannes Verlag, 1967.

'Mysterium Paschale', in *Mysterium Salutis*, J. Feiner and M. Lohrer, ed. Einsiedeln: Benziger Verlag, 1969; trans. as *Mysterium Paschale*, Aidan Nichols, OP, Edinburgh: T. and T. Clark, 1990.

Herrlichkeit. Eine theologische Aesthetik, III/2, 2. Teil: Neuer Bund, Einsiedeln: Johannes Verlag, 1969; trans. as *The Glory of the Lord, Vol. VII: Theology: The New Covenant*, Brian McNeil, Edinburgh: T. and T. Clark, 1989.

Einfaltungen, Munich: Koeel Verlag GmbH and Co., 1969.

160   *A Spiritual Theology of the Priesthood*

Klarstellungen, Freiburg-im-Breisgau: Verlag Herder KG, 1971; trans. as *Elucidations*. John Riches, London: SPCK, 1975.
In Gottes Einsatz leben, Einsiedeln: Johannes Verlag, 1971; trans. as *Engagement with God*, John Halliburton, London: SPCK, 1975.
Die Warheit ist symphonische, Einsiedeln: Johannes Verlag, 1972.
Der antiromische Affekt, Freiburg-im-Breisgau: Verlag Herder KG, 1974; trans. as *The Office of Peter and the Structure of the Church*, Andre Emery, San Francisco: Ignatius Press, 1986.
Pneuma und Institution. Skizzen zur Theologie, IV, Einsiedeln: Johannes Verlag, 1974.
Christlicher Stand, Einsiedeln: Johannes Verlag, 1977; trans. as *The Christian State of Life*, Sr Mary Frances McCarthy, San Francisco: Ignatius Press, 1983.
Theodramatik, II: Die Personen des Spieles, 2. Teil: Die Personen in Christus, Einsiedeln: Johannes Verlag, 1978; trans. as *Theodrama, Vol II: The Dramatis Personae: Man in God*, Graham Harrison, San Francisco: Ignatius Press, 1990.
Neue Klarstellungen, Einsiedeln: Johannes Verlag, 1979.
Kennt uns Jesus – Kennen wir ihn? Freiburg-im-Breisgau: Verlag Herder KG, 1980.
Theodramatik, III: Die Handlung, Einsiedeln: Johannes Verlag, 1980: trans. as *Theodrama, Vol. IV: The Action*, Graham Harrison, San Francisco: Ignatius Press, 1994.
Kleine Fibel für verunsicherte Laien, Einsiedeln: Johannes Verlag, 1980.
Unser Auftrag: Bericht und Entwurf, Einsiedeln: Johannes Verlag, 1984.
Was dürfen wir hoffen?, Einsiedeln: Johannes Verlag, 1986.
Mein Werk, Durchblicke, Einsiedeln: Johannes Verlag, 1990.

ARTICLES (IN ORDER OF PUBLICATION)

'Personne et Fonction', *Parole de Dieu et Sacerdoce*, Études presentées a S. Exc. Mgr. Weber, Archeveque-Eveque de Strasbourg (1962).
'Über das priesterliche Amt', *Civitas*, 23 (1960), pp. 794–797.
'From the Theology of God to the Theology of the Church', *Communio*, IX (1982), p. 195.
'Jesus and Forgiveness', *Communio*, XI (1984), pp. 322ff.
'The Holy Church and the Eucharistic Sacrifice', *Communio*, XII (1985), pp. 139ff.
'Theology and Holiness', *Communio*, XIV (1987), p. 341.
'The Marian Principle', *Communio*, XV (1988), p. 122.

SELECTED WORKS ABOUT BALTHASAR

Albus, M., *Die Warheit ist Liebe. Zur Unterscheidung des Christlichen bei H. Urs von Balthasar*, Freiburg: Herder, 1976.

Babini, E., *L'antropologia teologica di Hans Urs von Balthasar*, Milano: Jaca Book, 1987.

Dupré, L., 'Hans Urs von Balthasar's Theology of Aesthetic Form', *Theological Studies*, 49 (1988), pp. 299–318.

Faux, J. M., 'Un Theologien: Hans Urs von Balthasar', *Nouvelle Revue Theologique*, 94 (1972), pp. 1009–1030.

Ford, D., ed. *The Modern Theologians, Volume I*, Oxford: Basil Blackwell, 1989.

Guerriero, E., *Hans Urs von Balthasar*, Milano: Edizione Paoline, 1991.

Hemmerle, K., 'Das Neue ist älter: Hans Urs von Balthasar und die Orientierung der Theologie', *Erbe und Auftrag*, 57 (1981), pp. 81–98.

Henrici, P., 'Hans Urs von Balthasar: A Sketch of His Life', *Communio*, XVI (1989), pp. 306–350.

Houdijx, M., 'Une Discussion recente sur les fondements neo-testamentaires; de ministère sacerdotal', *Concilium*, 80 (1972), pp. 141–152.

Johri, M., *Descensus Dei. Teologia della Croce nell'opera di Hans Urs von Balthasar*, Roma, 1981.

Kay, J., 'Hans Urs von Balthasar: Theologien post-Critique?' *Concilium*, 161 (1981), pp. 141–148.

Kehl, M. and Loser, W., ed., *In der Fule des Glaubens: Hans Urs von Balthasar – Lesebuch*, Freiburg-im-Breisgau: Verlag Herder KG, 1980; trans. as *The Von Balthasar Reader*, Robert J. Daly, SJ Edinburgh: T. and T. Clark, 1982.

Krenst, Th. R., *Passio caritatis. Trinitarische Passiologie im Werke Hans Urs von Balthasar*, Einsiedeln-Freiburg: Johannes Verlag, 1990.

Lehman, K. and Kasper, W., *Hans Urs von Balthasar, Gestalt und Werk*, Colonia: Verlag für christliche Literatur Communio, 1989.

Löser, W., 'Unangefochtene Kirchlichkeit – universaler Horizont: Weg und Werk Hans Urs von Balthasars', *Herder Korrespondenz*, 42 (1988), pp. 472–479.

Marchesi, G., *La Cristologia di Hans Urs von Balthasar. La Figura di Gesu Cristo expressione visibile di Dio*, Roma, 1977.

McDade, J., 'Reading von Balthasar', *The Month*, 20 (1987), pp. 136–143.

McGregor, B., O.P. and Norris, T., ed., *The Beauty of Christ: An*

Introduction to the Theology of Hans Urs von Balthasar, Edinburgh: T. & T. Clark, 1994.

Moda, A., *Hans Urs von Balthasar. Un'esposizione critica del suo pensiero* Bari: Ecumenica Edizione, 1976.

Mooney, H., *The Liberation of Consciousness*, Bernard Lonergan's Theological Foundations in Dialogue with the Theological Aesthetics of Hans Urs von Balthasar, Frankfurt: Kencht, 1992.

Oakes, Edward, *Pattern of Redemption*, New York: Continuum, 1991.

O'Donnell, J., *Hans Urs von Balthasar*, London: Geoffrey Chapman, 1992.

— 'Hans Urs von Balthasar: The Form of His Theology', *Communio*, XVI (1989), pp. 458–474.

— 'The Trinity in Recent German Theology', *Heythrop Journal*, 123 (1982), pp. 115–167.

O'Donovan, L., 'God's Glory in Time', *Communio*, 2 (1975), pp. 250–269.

O'Hanlon, G., *The Immutability of God in the Theology of Hans Urs von Balthasar*, Cambridge: The University Press, 1990.

— 'The Jesuits and Modern Theology', *ITQ*, 58 (1992), pp. 25–45.

— Von Balthasar and Ecclesial States of Life', *Miltown Studies*, 22 (1988), p. 11–117.

Rahner, K., 'Hans Urs von Balthasar', *Civitas*, 20 (1965), pp. 601–604.

Riches, J., 'Hans Urs von Balthasar', in *The Modern Theologians*, ed. David F. Ford. Oxford: Blackwell, 1989.

— *The Analogy of Beauty*, Edinburgh: T. & T. Clark, 1986.

Ritt, P., 'The Lordship of Jesus Christ: Balthasar and Sobrino', *Theological Studies*, 49 (1988), pp. 709–731.

Roberts, L., *The Theological Aesthetics of Hans Urs von Balthasar*, Washington: Catholic University of America Press, 1987.

Roten, J., 'Marian Anthropological Dimensions in the Common Mission of Adrienne von Speyer and Hans Urs von Balthasar', *Communio*, XVI (1989), pp. 419–445.

Saward, J., *The Mysteries of March*, London: Collins, 1990.

Schindler, D.L., ed. *Hans Urs von Balthasar: His Life and Work*, San Francisco: Ignatius Press, Communio Books, 1991.

Sicari, A., 'Hans Urs von Balthasar: Theology and Holiness', *Communio*, XVI (1989), pp. 351–365.

Scola, A., *Hans Urs von Balthasar: A Theological Style*, Edinburgh: T. & T. Clark, 1991.

Vignolo, R., *Estetica e singolarità*, Milano: I. P. L., 1982.

Williams, R., 'Balthasar and Rahner', in *The Analogy of Beauty*, ed. John Riches. Edinburgh: T. & T. Clark, 1986.

SECONDARY WORKS

Alison, J., *Knowing Jesus*, London: SPCK, 1993.

Bernier, P., *Ministry and the Church*, Mystic, Conn.: Twenty-Third Publications, 1992.

Bouyer, L., *A History of Christian Spirituality, Vol. I: The Spirituality of the New Testament and the Fathers*, New York: Seabury Press, 1982.

— *Le Fils eternal*, Paris: Les Editions du Cerf, 1970).

— *Women in the Church*, San Francisco: Ignatius Press, 1982.

Brown, D., *Continental Philosophy and Modern Theology*, Oxford: Blackwell, 1987.

Brown, R., *Priest and Bishop*, London: Geoffrey Chapman, 1971.

Burrows, D. P., 'The Feast of Sukkoth in Rabbinic and Related Literature', unpub. diss., Cincinnati, Ohio: Hebrew Union College – Jewish Institute of Religion, May, 1974.

Chantraine, G., 'Apostolicity according to Schillebeeckx', *Communio*, XV (1988).

Cochini, C., SJ, *Origines Apostoliques du Celibat Sacerdotal*, Paris: Editions Lethielleur, 1980.

Colson, J., *Ministre de Jésus-Christ ou Le Sacerdoce de l'Evangile*, Paris: Editions du Cerf, 1966.

Congar, Y., *I Believe in the Holy Spirit, Vol. II: The Lord and Giver of Life*, London: Geoffrey Chapman, 1983.

Cooke, B., *Ministry to Word and Sacraments*, Philadelphia: Fortress Press, 1976.

Copens, J., *Sacerdoce et Celibat*, Gembloux: Editions Duculot, S.A., 1971.

Delorme, J. ed., *Le Ministère et Les Ministères selon Le Nouveau Testament*, Seuil: Parole de Dieu, 1974.

deLubac, H., *Les églises particulières dans l'Église universelle, suivi de La maternité de l'église*, Paris: Aubier Montaigne, 1971.

Dulles, Avery, 'Models for Ministerial Priesthood', *Origins*, 20 (1990), pp. 284–289.

— *Catholicity of the Church*, Oxford: Clarendon Press, 1988.

— *Models of the Church*, New York: Doubleday, 1974.

Dunn, J. D. G., *Christology in the Making*. London: SCM Press, 1980.

— *Jesus and the Spirit*, London: SCM Press, 1975.

— *The Parting of the Ways*, London: SCM Press, 1991.

Dunn, P., *Priesthood*, New York: Alba House, 1990.

Favale, A., *Il Ministero presbyterale: Aspetti dottrinali, pastorali, spirituali*, Roma: Libreria Ateneo Salesiano, 1989.

Flannery, A., ed., *Documents of Vatican Council II*, Collegeville, Minnesota: Liturgical Press, 1975.

Galot, J., *The Theology of the Priesthood*, San Francisco: Ignatius Press, 1985.

Girard, R., *Violence and the Sacred*, Baltimore and London: Johns Hopkins University Press, 1977.

— *Things Hidden Since the Foundation of the World*, London: Athlone Press, 1987.

— *The Scapegoat*, London: Athlone Press, 1986.

Grelot, P., *Église et ministères: Pour un dialogue critique avec Edward Schillebeeckx*, Paris: Cerf, 1983.

Greshake, G., *The Meaning of Christian Priesthood*, Dublin: Four Courts Press, 1988.

Hastings, A., *Modern Catholicism*, London: SPCK, 1991.

Hayter, M., *The New Eve in Christ*, London: SPCK, 1987.

Hengel, M., *Between Jesus and Paul*, London: SCM Press, 1983.

— *The Cross of the Son of God*, London: SCM Press, 1986.

— *The Pre-Christian Paul*, London: SCM Press, 1991.

Heschel, A. J., *God in Search of Man*, (New York: Harper and Row, 1955.

Hume, B., *Light in the Lord. Reflections on Priesthood*, Slough: St Paul Publications, 1991.

International Theological Commission, *Texts and Documents, 1969–1985*, San Francisco: Ignatius Press, 1989.

John Paul II, *A Priest Forever*, Dublin: Veritas, 1982.

— *Pastores Dabo Vobis*, London: Catholic Truth Society, 1992.

Jüngel, G., *The Doctrine of the Trinity*, Edinburgh: Scottish Academic Press, 1976.

— *The Mystery of God at the Heart of the World*, Edinburgh: T. & T. Clark, 1983.

Kasper, W., 'Die Funktion des Priesters in der Kirche', *Geist und Leben*, 42 (1969), pp. 102–106.

— *The God of Jesus Christ*, London: SCM Press, 1984.

— *Theology and Church*, London: SCM Press, 1989.

— 'Ministry in the Church: Taking Issue with Edward Schillebeeckx', *Communio*, 10 (1983), pp. 185–195.

Kee, A., ed., *Being and Truth: Essays in Honour of John Macquarrie*, London: SCM Press, 1986.

Kehl, M., *Die Kirche: Eine Katholische Ekklesiologia*, Würzburg: Echter Verlag, 1992.

Keyes, P., *Pastoral Presence and the Diocesan Priest*, Whitinsville, Mass.: Affirmation House, 1978.

Kilmartin, E. J., 'Apostolic Office: Sacrament of Christ', *Theological Studies*, 36 (1975), p. 261.

Larkin, E., *Spiritual Renewal of the American Priesthood*, Washington, D.C.: U.S. Catholic Conference, 1973.

Lauder, R., *The Priest as Person*, Whitinsville, Mass.: Affirmation House, 1981.

Mackinnon, D., *Themes in Theology*, Edinburgh: T. & T. Clark, 1987.

Macquarrie, J., *Jesus Christ in Modern Thought*, London: SCM Press, 1990.

— *The Humility of God*, London: SCM Press, 1978.

— *Theology, Church and Ministry*, London: SCM Press, 1986.

Martelet, G., *Deux Mille Ans d'Église en Question*, Paris: Editions du Cerf, Vol. 1, 1984; Vols. 2 and 3, 1990.

Martini, C., *The Testimony of St Paul*. Slough: St Paul Publications, 1981.

Mascall, E., *Theology and the Gospel of Christ*, London: SPCK, 1977.

Masure, E., *The Diocesan Priest: A Study in the Theological Spirituality of the Priesthood*, London: Chapman, 1957.

McBrien, R., *Ministry*, San Francisco: Harper and Row, 1987.

McDade, J., 'The Continuing Reality of the Jewish Covenant', *The Month*, Sept./Oct. (1991), pp. 370–382.

McGregor, B. and Norris, T., ed., *The Formation Journey of the Priest: Exploring 'Pastores Dabo Vobis'*, Dublin: Columba Press, 1994.

Marmion, C., *Christ the Ideal of the Priest*, London: Sands and Co., 1952.

Martos, J., *Doors to the Sacred*, London: SCM Press, 1981.

Moltmann, J., *History and the Triune God*, London: SCM Press, 1991.

— *The Crucified God*, London: SCM Press, 1974.

— *The Passion for Life – A Messianic Lifestyle*, Philadelphia: Fortress Press, 1978.

— *The Power of the Powerless*, London: SCM Press, 1982.

— *The Trinity and the Kingdom of God*, London: SCM Press, 1981.

Moule, C. F. D., *The Origins of Christology*, Cambridge: The University Press, 1977.

Navone, J., *Self-Giving and Sharing*, Collegeville, Minnesota: The Liturgical Press, 1989).

Nichols, A., *Holy Order*, Dublin: Veritas, 1990.

Nouwen, H., *Intimacy*, Notre Dame, Ind.: Fides Claretian, 1969.

— *The Wounded Healer*, New York: Doubleday, 1972.

O'Collins, G., *Interpreting Jesus*, London: Chapman, 1983.

— *Jesus Risen*, London: Darton, Longman and Todd, 1987.

166   *A Spiritual Theology of the Priesthood*

— *The Calvary Christ*, London: SCM Press, 1977.

O'Donnell, J., *The Mystery of the Triune God*, London: Heythrop, 1988.

—*Trinity and Temporality*, Oxford: The University Press, 1983.

O'Meara, T., *A Theology of Ministry*, New York: Paulist Press, 1988.

Osborne, K., *Priesthood: A History of the Ordained Ministry in the Roman Catholic Church*, New York: Paulist Press, 1988.

Pennington, B., *The Eucharist Yesterday and Today*, Slough: St Paul Publications, 1984.

Power, D., *The Christian Priest: Elder and Prophet*, London: Sheed and Ward, 1973.

Perri, W. D., *A Radical Challenge for Priesthood Today*, Mystic, Conn.: Twenty-Third Publications, 1996.

Rahner, K., 'Der Glaube des Priesters Heute', *Geist und Leben*, 40 (1967), pp. 269–285.

— *Servants of the Lord*, London: Burns and Oates, 1968.

Ramsey, M., *The Christian Priest*, London: SPCK, 1972.

Ratzinger, J., 'The Formation of Priests in the Circumstances of the Present Day,' *Communio*, XVI (1990), pp. 626ff.

— *Ministers of Your Joy*, Slough: St Paul Publications, 1988.

Richards, Michael, *A People of Priests*, London: Darton, Longman and Todd, 1975.

Rosato, P., 'The Spirituality of the Diocesan Priest', *The Way Supplement*, 39 (1980).

— 'The Sacrament of Orders', in Walsh, M., ed. *Commentary on the Catechism of the Catholic Church*, London: Geoffrey Chapman, 1994, pp. 303–317.

Rowley, H. H., *The Faith of Israel*, London, SCM Press, 1956.

Schillebeeckx, E., *The Church with a Human Face*, New York: Crossroad, 1985.

— *Church: The Human Story of God*, London: SCM Press, 1990.

— *Ministry: Leadership in the Community of Jesus Christ*, New York: Crossroad, 1991.

Schreiter, R., *The Schillebeeckx Reader*, Edinburgh: T. & T. Clark, 1986.

Schwager, R., *Must There Be Scapegoats? Violence and Redemption in the Bible*, San Francisco: Harper and Row, 1987.

Sobrino, J., *Christology at the Crossroads*, London: SCM Press, 1978.

— *Spirituality of Liberation*, New York: Orbis, 1988.

Spiegel, S., *The Last Trial*, New York: Schocken Books, 1967.

Stanley, D., *Jesus in Gethsemane*, New York: Paulist Press, 1982.

— 'Call to Discipleship', *The Way Supplement*, January (1982)

Sykes, S. W., *Sacrifice and Redemption*, Cambridge: The University Press, 1991.

Tavard, G. H., *A Theology for Ministry*, Wilmington: Michael Glazier, 1983.

Taylor, V., *The Names of Jesus*, London: MacMillan, 1954.

Terwilliger, R., *To Be a Priest*, New York: Seabury, 1975.

Torrance, T., *The Incarnation*, Edinburgh: The Handsel Press, 1981.

Vanhoye, A., 'Le Ministère dans l'Église: Les données du nouveau testament,' *Nouvelle Revue Théologique* 114 (1982), pp. 122–138.

— 'Sacerdoce commun et sacerdoce ministériel: Distinctions et rapports,' *Nouvelle Revue Théologique* 107 (1975).

— *Old Testament Priests and the New Priest*, Petersham, Mass.: St Bede Publications, 1986.

— *Our Priest is Christ*, Roma, 1977.

Vanstone, W., *Love's Endeavour, Love's Expense*, London: Darton, Longman and Todd, 1971.

Vogels, H., *Celibacy – Gift or Law?*, Tunbridge Wells, Kent: Burns & Oates/Search Press Ltd., 1992.

Williams, R., *The Wound of Knowledge*, London: Darton, Longman and Todd, 1990.

Wuerl, D., *The Priesthood*, Rome: Angelicum University, 1979.

INDEX OF NAMES

INDEX OF SUBJECTS